TRANSFORMING DAMASCUS

Leila Hudson is Assistant Professor in the Departments of Near Eastern Studies, History, and Anthropology at the University of Arizona.

TRANSFORMING DAMASCUS
Space and Modernity in an Islamic City

LEILA HUDSON

Tauris Academic Studies
LONDON • NEW YORK

Published in 2008 by Tauris Academic Studies,
an imprint of I.B. Tauris & Co Ltd
6 Salem Road, London W2 4BU
175 Fifth Avenue, New York NY 10010
www.ibtauris.com

In the United States of America and Canada distributed by
Palgrave Macmillan, a division of St. Martin's Press
175 Fifth Avenue, New York NY 10010

Library of Middle East History 16

ISBN: 978 1 84511 579 1

A full CIP record for this book is available from the British Library
A full CIP record for this book is available from the Library of Congress

Library of Congress catalog card: available

Printed and bound in India by Thomson Press India Limited
camera-ready copy edited and supplied by the author

For my mother,
Vera Wahbe Hudson
(1936–2007)

CONTENTS

ACKNOWLEDGMENTS

Research for this study was made possible by funding from the Social Science Research Council, the Fulbright Hays program, and a Hewlett Grant for European Archival Research. I would like to thank the late Mme. Da'd Hakim, who presided over the archives at the *Markaz lil Watha'iq al-Tarikhiyya* in Suq Saruja, Damascus, in the 1990s and her able successor Dr. Ghassan 'Ubayd. I would also like to thank Dr. Akram 'Ulabi, who knows the *shari'a* court archives of Damascus like no one else; Dr. Nazih Kawakibi for his walking tours of the hidden sites of Islamic Damascus; Dr. K. Qasimiya for her insights into power and politics; and Dr. Abd al-Razzaq Mo'az, whose knowledge of architecture and sharing of his father's photographic archive extended back far before his service to his country as deputy minister of culture. The late Dr. Selim Barakat was an invaluable guide to the Arabic books and manuscripts of the nineteenth century. I am also grateful to James Gelvin, the late Hanna Batatu, 'Abdallah Hanna, Linda Schilcher, Elizabeth Picard, Leila Fawaz, Andrew Vincent, and most especially Abdul-Karim Rafeq for their advice and support over the years. I am grateful to David, Tatiana, and Susannah Butter for putting me up in London, to Dr. Ra'if Khoury of the Orientalische Facultät of the University of Heidelberg, and to Dr. Majid Fakhry and the late Hisham Sharabi of Georgetown University for sharing their university work facilities with me. My colleagues at the University of Arizona, especially Carl Smith and Julia Clancy-Smith, provided me with valuable encouragement and advice. Linda Darling, Randi Deguilhem, Tad Park, Jens Hanssen, and Itzchak Weismann provided very helpful feedback. Many thanks are due to Leila Muzarza' and her extended family for opening their homes to me and teaching me the subtleties of Damascus culture and Islam. Michael, Vera, and Aida Hudson have been a source of patient support from the onset to the end. Riad, Zayna, and Zayd Altoubal bore the brunt of the writing of this study, and I thank them for helping me bring it to closure.

TRANSFORMING DAMASCUS

1

BAB AL-SHAM:
APPROACHING DAMASCUS

Introduction

In the half century between 1860 and World War I, Damascus changed from a provincial center of the Ottoman Empire to the capital city of a nation-state in formation. During that time, we see the emergence of the cluster of changes we associate with modernity. Secular values of national identity began to seriously challenge the religious traditions that had structured the past. New technologies and Western styles made inroads, and goods and ideas flowed in from the West at new rates. The state centralized and increased its power, and individuals began to clamor for rights and representation not as subjects of an empire, but as citizens. How did this transformation occur?

Recent attempts to pin down Syrian modernity have come up short.[1] To encompass simultaneously "the impact of global modernity" as it was "appropriated, adapted or resisted" and "the ways business was conducted in the increasingly cosmopolitan and complex cities of the time, where both commodities and ideas were exchanged"[2] requires an acknowledgment of plural modernities, multiple pathways of transformation even within a single city. Many story lines converge in urban space and coincide in a time when outside pressures reached a critical level and a critical number of forms and avenues.

This complex historical transformation has most often been approached as linear, natural, and incomplete by modernization theorists and Arab nationalist historians alike. The former generally attribute progress to European influences and setbacks to Oriental backwardness;[3] the latter attribute progress to national awakening and setbacks to imperial meddling.[4] The process of transformation of Damascus, however (or of any other complex social and cultural system, for that matter), was not linear but manifold. It was not the organic development of a predestined collectivity but rather was the result of many different processes in which people (both powerful and ordinary) manipulated the various values in their lives—material wealth, family, learning, and power—to prepare for an uncertain future in an uncharted and unpredictable world in which global forces played an increasingly important role.

A book written by a family team of Damascene notables between 1890 and 1900 testifies in substance and form to the incorporation of Damascus into an economy beyond its ken and to the transition from a religious to an anxiously global worldview. The *Qamus al-Sina'at al-Shamiyya* (Dictionary of Damascene Craft and Industry), with entries for 437 crafts, provides a glimpse into the local economic changes of the late nineteenth century.[5] In describing the landscape of work and manufacturing at the end of the century, it includes observations about the changing times. For example, a major enterprise emphasizing Damascus's primary orientation to the geography of Islam was the *muqawwim* (literally, "entrepreneur"), which outfitted the annual influx of pilgrims for the grueling weeks-long overland trip to Medina and Mecca. This industry was clearly accustomed to high risks and returns, but by the end of the nineteenth century the *muqawwim* began to face a different type of challenge.

> *Muqawwim:* Those who provide all services for travel to the Hijaz for those who wish to visit the two noble *harams* of Mecca and Medina. The practitioner of this industry must have a sufficient number of camels at his disposal and all the necessities in good provision that is: tents and hardware, beds . . . as well as servants. And when the season of the hajj arrives, the *muqawwim* approaches those who need to travel. And whoever wants to go on the hajj rents from him what he needs for the ride, in terms of food from Damascus to Medina or Mecca, each according to his own means. This is an important industry with a broad range of business and requires a large amount of capital. Whoever profits, profits well indeed and whoever loses, loses a monstrous amount. And this industry is about to turn a new page and that because of the predicted arrival of the railroad to the two holy cities. And that is from the kindness of great God, to whom we are grateful.[6]

The early-twentieth-century Hijaz Railway connection between Damascus and Medina was in the end a rather minor challenge to the business of the hajj pilgrimage, following the far more serious introduction of steamship travel decades earlier and the opening of the Suez Canal in 1869, which diverted the overland trade to much safer water routes.7 New systems of transport, as we will see, were catalysts of regional economic and cultural change. Paved roads, railways, and water travel were the prerequisites for the commercial links to the Mediterranean coast that would undermine the established regional patterns of industry far more extensively. As the Qasimis documented, weavers, spinners and cloth printers were among those most dramatically affected by European imports. Of the plight of Damascene weavers and cloth printers, Muhammad Saʿid al-Qasimi wrote,

[B]ut cloths imported from European countries boggle the mind, and these are worked on innumerable looms, but then this book is about Damascene industry and those that are living from it, and God is the opener of doors, the cause of all effects, and he is the gift and the giver. . . .

This craft used to be very profitable in Damascus. But now, due to the imports of printed cloth of all patterns and kinds from foreign countries, this industry has reached the point of stagnation. Its practitioners are few in Damascus. And nobody wants printed cloth anymore except for peasant women who continue to wear their traditional costumes.8

The Qasimi dictionary also documents the coming of new occupations, for example,

Khardaji—Those who deal in many diverse products most coming from far away countries, like the land of the francs, Istanbul or nearby places like Beirut. They deal in innumerable objects, European products—and these are the majority—too many to list, such as the products of the factories of all kinds—utensils, glass products, all kinds of iron—scissors, knives, needles, and more and hand made Istanbul goods like combs, spoons and other handmade goods which I will not go into in detail because the aim of this book is to gather together the industries and crafts of Damascus which people here depend on, and nothing else.9

In addition to the economic changes that occurred as Damascus was bypassed and reconnected to other regions by new transport routes, cultural changes are also apparent in the *Qamus*. The project and authorship of

Qamus al-Sina'at al-Shamiyya itself gives evidence of a shift in the interests of religious scholars and the beginnings of the formation of a regional consciousness that is not yet national, but rather reflects local anxiety about threats to the traditional way of life. The primary author, the primary instigator, and the editor of the *Qamus* represent three generations of a prominent family of religious scholars in Damascus, the Qasimi family. Muhammad Sa'id al-Qasimi, the primary author, lived between 1843 and 1900. Trained as a religious scholar in the tradition of his own father, he preached and led prayers at the Sinaniyya and Hasaniyya mosques for most of his adult life. Yet he also wrote poetry and compiled this ethnographic study of his city's economy. His son, Jamal al-Din, who encouraged him to begin the work on Damascus and apparently sponsored Khalil al-'Azm's completion of the work after Muhammad Sa'id's death, was also religiously trained, but, as we will see, was a key transitional figure in using the principle of *ijtihad,* or religious innovation, to pave the way for religious reform and early national identity. And the fact that the work was largely completed by Muhammad Sa'id's son-in-law, Khalil al-'Azm—who was not a jurist but rather the scion of a prominent and powerful Damascene family—underlines the gradual shift from exclusively religious to more worldly perspectives.

The book uses the classical Arabic literary format of the entry-based encyclopedia in conjunction with the modern scientific-sounding appellation of dictionary (*qamus*).[10] Jamal al-Din is said to have suggested to his father that the latter begin at the southern extreme of the city and make his way systematically northward, recording all the different types of work he encountered. In this we see the development of a new style, a focus on new values of observation and description. The book is written in nonrhymed prose on the whole, and most sections end with an invocation of God's power. As was seen in the previous citations, the inquiry led to forms of work closely linked to the world outside Damascus, yet the author struggled not to be drawn away from his subject—that which provided the livelihood of the people of Damascus. In a sense, then, the emergence of a local anxiety was in part a response to the encroaching products of the outside world.

Cultural Change as the Production of Space

The French geographer Henri Lefebvre suggested in the 1970s that we approach cultural change in terms of what he called "the production of space." Arguing that historiography tended to portray change as a linear unfolding of narrative in time, Lefebvre directed attention to the architecture, cities, and environment that are both the product and the setting of human action and the repository of investments of wealth and energy. Lefebvre's approach emphasizes that the space of the city is made and shaped by people, that it is not empty or neutral Cartesian space but bursting with compound meanings and stories, and that its exploration is necessary to understand culture and history in anything other than abstractions.[11] Investigating the transformation from a provincial to a national city in terms of Lefebvre's concept of the production of space helps avoid the traps of customary linear approaches to history, with their familiar narratives of great and tragic heroes and naturalized trajectories of social development. The changing city is at least a plane on which many structures are built and many parallel and intersecting stories are lived, often undocumented. Better yet is the image of urban space as a volume in which leaves or levels are laid down over time, superimposed, concealing, but interpenetrated and pregnant with discrete and interwoven meanings.

Lefebvre wrote in the 1970s of a critical analysis that would analyze a house not as "the epitome of immovability" but as defined by that which flowed through it:

> The house is permeated from every direction by streams of energy which run in and out of it by every imaginable route: water, gas, electricity, telephone lines, radio and television signals, and so on. Its image of immovability would then be replaced by an image of a complex of mobilities, a nexus of in and out conduits. . . . By depicting this convergence of waves and currents, this new image, much more accurately than any drawing or photograph, would at the same time disclose the fact that this piece of "immovable property" is actually a . . . machine.[12]

Any city, in this case Damascus, is (like Lefebvre's house and all other places of interest) a nexus of flows. But unlike the house with its defining walls and roof, the city cannot be characterized (after Le Corbusier's famous dictum) as a simply functional machine with binary in and out circuits. A city is a system in which "in" and "out" were not clear even in the age when the ancient walls had a real protective function. The number and type of currents are daunting, and the question of internal circulation or order cannot be neglected.

The resources and forms of cultural capital in question, whose movement shapes urban environment and culture, vary in type and texture from the barely perceptible subtleties of family prestige to gold and military matériel. In focusing on resource circulation, my method seeks to discern new patterns of accumulation and exploitation of those resources associated with modernity. The idea of cultures of circulation has been developed as part of an anthropology of fast-moving contemporary international cities and financial forms; it is equally useful for the understanding of cities and of historical change more generally.[13]

Dynamics of Cultural Capital Movement

The nature of a place—from a house, to a body, to a village, to a nation-state—is determined by the types and patterns of circulation of currents flowing through the system; and changes in these current types and movement patterns are the basis of the integral shaping or reshaping of a system. The reshaping of a system occurs in three different ways. Some structures are formed by capital-intensive earth-moving projects. Others are formed like paths by the incidental passing of many feet in the same direction. Still others are formed by the undirected infusion of liquidity from outside the system.

As anyone who has undertaken the most superficial adjustments to his or her own lived environment knows, the process of intentionally redesigning spaces and places is expensive, disruptive, and draining. It can be hugely rewarding if successful, but it is also full of unseen possible outcomes. The enterprise of such projects is one of the key ways space is produced—by risky but rewarding initiatives on the part of those with sufficient (or apparently sufficient) resources.

This is not the only way space is shaped, however. Much of space, particularly during earlier eras, has been shaped without intention, almost imperceptibly, by many low-stakes decisions. At colleges and universities with large lawns and quadrangles, for example, students would bypass the paved sidewalks that were designed by architects to enhance the lines of the campus. Over time, the students simply wore paths in the quadrangles, cutting diagonal patterns as they moved repeatedly from dormitory to classroom to dining hall. Simply paving the paths worn by the students' movements after the fact was a more effective way to make sidewalks. The trails or paths made by this kind of patterned movement are an important, and overlooked, way in which collective space is shaped. Thoroughfares, traffic patterns, markets, and recreational spaces tend to be established gradually by many anonymous, low-risk decisions about how to spend minor resources.

The third way to shape the environment is by the sudden and unexpected introduction of elements or energy from outside the immediate locale.

Like a flood, landslide, or wildfire in nature, an invading army, an influx of refugees, a plethora of imports dumped into the system, a new currency, or a windfall profit or gift can have immediate, dramatic, and far-reaching consequences on a physical and cultural environment. Moreover, its effects may shape the landscape for a long time to come.

Each of these modes of production of space is the result of the movement of resources. Significant streams of different kinds of currencies of cultural capital passing through the environment are the primary mechanism of the production of space. Where they pass or are exchanged becomes a thoroughfare, market, or commons. Where they are marshaled, concentrated, and stored becomes an investment. Where they flood and pool becomes a challenge, a watershed, or an opportunity for change. While we focus here on resource or capital flows as the immediate mechanism of transformation, what we are ultimately interested in is reevaluating the role of human action in the process.

Currencies of Cultural Capital

The resources that circulate in a system and shape it are not restricted to economic values of money or commodities. I use the concept of cultural capital to include, alongside financial capital, other forms of cultural assets that are not immediately consumed but can be accumulated and are available for the production of more value. As understood here, cultural capital means the general category of all that is most valuable in a society over the long term. One of Pierre Bourdieu's most provocative and intriguing ideas in *Outline of a Theory of Practice* is one of his simplest and suggests a new way of understanding political economy:

> Thus the theory of strictly economic practice is simply a particular case of a general theory of the economics of practice. The only way to escape from the ethnocentric naïvetés of economism, without falling into populist exaltation of the generous naïveté of earlier forms of society, is to carry out in full what economics does only partially, and to extend economic calculation to all the goods, material and symbolic, without distinction, that present themselves as rare and worthy of being sought after in a particular social formation—which may be "fair words" or smiles, handshakes or shrugs, compliments or attention, challenges or insults, honour or honours, powers or pleasures, gossip or scientific information, distinction or distinctions, etc.[14]

The project suggested by Bourdieu is no less than the attempt to embed the study of economics, theoretically and historically, into the ethnographic study of cultural values—not static or typical, but circulating. I focus here primarily on the subset of cultural capital forms that were systematically documented in the sources available to a historian of Damascus. The types of cultural capital I consider are those suggested by the textual artifacts I unearthed: property, money, family, knowledge, and imperial and local power.

Bourdieu's vision, sometimes obscured by a subtlety and complexity that make communication difficult, presents an alternative to the Marxian and Weberian paradigms that have oriented historical anthropology. Marxian and Weberian approaches both import theories of European social change to explain apparent stagnation in extra-European contexts.

Karl Marx understood the cultural area of which Syria is a part as dominated by the Asiatic mode of production and irrigation-linked Oriental despotism. According to Marx, the absence of ownership in such a system resulted in the absence of class and consequently the class struggle that fuels historical change. For Marx, therefore, change must be imported from outside the system, through commerce or imperialism. Like Marx, Max Weber sees Middle Eastern change in negative terms. The factors that produced rationalization in Europe are absent; therefore any social change must be brought about by charismatic rebellion, which leaves social structures untouched. For Marx and Weber, an Islamic city like Damascus is marked by the absence of European medieval autonomy and the corresponding corporated and juridical life, the absence of "real" feudal relations, "real" ownership and possession, industrialization and class struggle.

Unlike both Marx and Weber, Bourdieu began his own theoretical work in the "East" of postcolonial North Africa and moved west to the European metropole. More substantively, Bourdieu's schema, like that of Ibn Khaldun but in contrast to Marx and Weber, does not depend on a concept of total ownership rights or essential possession. While a Marxian historical materialism depends on a clear concept of private property (and a labor theory of value), and a Weberian typology depends on the scientific assignment of specific properties (in the sense of characteristics) to societies and cultures and status groups, Bourdieu's symbolic capital depends on practical exchange and misrecognition for the creation of value. For Bourdieu, the lack of well-defined ownership rights and the lack of class structures in Islamic culture do not present a problem. The question is not how ownership rights or other kinds of essence empower or fuel organic historical development, but rather how transitory possession and movement of values in space and time shape a complex social environment. Unlike Marxian or Weberian approaches, which lend themselves to understanding how non-European cities deviate from a naturalized Western-style capitalism, a Bourdieuian or Khaldunian approach traces the paths of exchange and suggests how "mere" passing of goods carves out a society's organizing structures and meanings.[15]

An Erosion Model of Resource Flows

Thus, the transformation of the city was the cumulative result of changes in the patterns of movement of the various values, or cultural capital, that the people of the city accumulated, spent, exchanged, imported, and exported in the process of living their lives and strategizing for an uncertain future. Changing patterns in how people spent and saved their money and goods are very important, but so are the paths carved out by the building of family relations, the circulation of knowledge through the city, and the exercise of different forms of political power.

As a fixed location on an evolving landscape, late Ottoman Damascus was shaped by what we might think of as the erosive effects of patterned resource flows of different forms of value. My erosion model is based loosely on one suggested by James Ferguson in his analysis of wealth in a village in Lesotho.[16] Rejecting the unidimensional developmental models that flourished in African studies, Ferguson suggests that different forms of wealth (money, cattle, sons, and daughters) that are not easily comparable or convertible because exchange is culturally and politically structured define a three-dimensional terrain of wealth. He writes:

> The attempt to locate households economically in such a setting thus requires mapping a politicocultural "topography" of channels facilitating the flow of commodity exchange, dams obstructing, slowing or filtering it, and furrows temporarily diverting the flow from one channel or dam into another. A meaningful ranking of wealthholding must include a cultural analysis of commodity paths and the structure of property.[17]

To push Ferguson's model one step further, the topography he suggests is not merely an analytical tool for comparing different households' wealth. The map of paths, channels, dams, and value flows provides a new perspective on the culture of that place as a whole—a new kind of model, different from the default model of structuralism and poststructuralism of a house that eventually imprisons its builders. This topographic model and concern with the city as a place makes the inquiry an archaeology of sorts, in that it starts with a geographical location, a place, and uses the tracks of history inscribed on that place as its data set and starting point for analysis and narrative. Following the tracks of urban structures and of archives over planar space can reveal the layout of the paths and channels—an overview of the system. The third dimension of a topographical map, depth, provides information about how much energy—hegemonic power or potential resistance—is invested in its structures and formations.

The structured and circuitous route in any particular culture by which money can be converted into other (more honorable) forms of good and vice versa is an obstacle course that only the society's most skillful members completely master. The particular timing, spacing, and conceptualization of the links and barriers between the economic and the noneconomic (and also among various forms of nonmonetary value) form the distinctive identity of a society and its culture. The absence of total convertibility of values at any point in time in an open and evolving system is the texture of its culture and friction of its history. From a traditional economic perspective, the reconciled bottom line is the important fact. In anthropological history, the route, the journey, and the terrain on the way to the "bottom line" constitute the important data.

The transformation of the landscape of Damascus was the result of many varied actors locally managing the cultural capital they could control to minimize risk and maximize value in response to the uncertainty that was the overriding symptom of the late nineteenth century pressures on the Ottoman Empire and its regional subsystems. The circulation of these resources shaped the urban system. We see the city and its spaces and institutions change, sometimes dramatically, more often very gradually, resulting in what we recognize as the qualitative changes of modernity. The mechanism for the changes includes a wide range of actions, from unrecorded decisions by ordinary Damascenes about whom to marry and what to name children to major, capital-intensive public works projects and military campaigns undertaken by the society's most powerful officials and businessmen and closely watched and documented by international observers.

Alternative Sources of Data

The relevance of such works as the *Qamus al-Sina'at al-Shamiyya* notwithstanding, it is important to look beyond the production of literature and other authored narratives—an almost exclusively elite, male practice that came to be dominated by those committed to modernization—at the role of the nonelites in the transformation. This project began with the premise that the bulk of the writings of a society's literate elites would only tell about one facet of modernity—modernity as a project of will by those elites. Ordinary people, women, the poor—those who did not inhabit the front lines of modernization and Westernization—were also subject to and objects of the changing regime and would have different stories to tell. How did they, too, contribute to or resist the city's transformation? We do not have their own life stories or words to tell us.

To approach the reshaping of Damascus in a systematic way, I sought out sources that traced the processes of the past beyond just the literature produced by modernist elites. These latter sources have been well studied in a way that tends to naturalize modernization, conflate modernity with modernism, and attribute a powerful causal will to that minority that produced articulate manifestos or even accounts of modernism.[18] The alternative sources, which help account for the emergence of modernist elites without depending on the modernists' testimony alone, are Islamic court records and the city and state infrastructures themselves.

The information recorded in probate inventories of the Islamic *shari'a* (Islamic law) court system of Damascus can help trace the movement and circulation of different currencies of value in the city. The records produced when a person's estate was divided according to the strict observance of Islamic law give us a set of data about the patterned order by which material wealth, human relationships, learning, and the new powers of the state were changing in the city of Damascus. Thus, we will use the probate documents—the Islamic bottom line, in which property, kin, and status are brought into a single document—to examine the changes in the distribution, circulation, and accumulation of these different forms of value (property, kin, knowledge, and power) during the critical period at the end of the Ottoman Empire.

Another way to access the patterns traced by streams and waves of capital is through the urban structures they created in this period. Thus, a second primary source for this project is the city of Damascus and the province around it. While trying to reconstruct private lives and private wealth of a late-Ottoman city in the Islamic court archives, I began to inquire into the histories encrypted in major public building projects that lined the streets I walked on my way to the archives in downtown Damascus. These buildings and the streets themselves, like the sometimes frustratingly idiosyncratic *shari'a* court archives, were the durable traces of political, economic, and cultural negotiations and investments. Many dated not from the French mandate period (1922–1945), where I was primed to look for modernity, but from the late-Ottoman period (1870s–1918). The streets, public works, councils, schools, squares, and railroads were investments in publicness. I found detailed narrative accounts of the modernization of the city in the British consular archival record, a source that links the projects to politics in detailed, almost ethnographic style, reflecting the urgency of the advanced imperial project of the "Eastern question." The British consuls, with an imperial interest in a renegade but not a strong Syria, monitored and surveyed Ottoman politics as the Ottomans sought to survey the province's unruly populace.

Organization

I have structured my chapters around broad categories of cultural capital. These chapters can be thought of in the architectural sense as *abwab*, or gates, as the chapters of a book are called in Arabic. Starting with a category of cultural capital, I have looked for patterns that tell a story and reveal part of the process of how Damascus was transformed by the actions of the ordinary and the powerful. Each chapter focuses on a different type of cultural capital and illuminates a different social dynamic. The book begins with chapter 2, *Bab al-Hukm*, in which the political capital of the Tanzimat reforms was introduced to Damascus by its Ottoman governors and carved out new spaces for popular expression. Before moving on to the trends in the movement of money, people, and knowledge among the general population, chapter 3, *Bab al-Wathaʾiq*, introduces the archival resources I used. In chapter 4, *Bab al-Mal*, I turn to the nineteenth-century reorientation of the Damascene economy to the Mediterranean coast and the subsequent liquidity that made new inroads into Damascus and allowed wealth stratification. In chapter 5, *Bab al-Usra*, we see how that liquidity, in conjunction with Islamic family dynamics, flowed into and produced a new middle class in which adaptation of old and new elements would flourish. In chapter 6, *Bab al-ʿIlm*, the focus on the contents of private libraries suggests the parameters of local religious and political discourse that underlay the new public sphere and shows how Islamic learning and practice became an increasingly potent form of cultural value at the century's end. Chapter 7, *Bab al-Watan*, focuses on how the broad political trends of centralization and decentralization that arose in the late Hamidian period were played out in investment in education and public works—particularly railroad projects. Chapter 8, *Bab al-Harb*, examines the depreciation of the political capital of the preceding periods as "turkification" bypassed Damascene political capital and as wartime Damascus was drained of cultural capital in several domains by desperate and failed Young Turk policies. None of these narratives alone is the single cause of the transformation of Damascus; together they create a fuller picture of a complex, dynamic system in which the actions of the powerful and the ordinary shape history and space.

2

BAB AL-HUKM: ON POLITICAL CAPITAL, 1860–1880

In the summer of 1860, the Christian section of Damascus was beset by gangs of thugs who killed, looted, and burned. Thousands of Christian residents of the eastern areas of the city were killed. Some took refuge with prominent Muslim citizens who shielded them, but many were defenseless against the onslaught. The perpetrators were an assortment of urban Muslim youths, Druze gangs from the hinterland, and tribal Bedouins, and the Muslim leadership of the city did little to stop them. Linked to similar disturbances in Mt. Lebanon, the rioting and killing belied a long history of Muslim/Christian coexistence in Damascus. Historians have seen the ugly incident as a turning point in the city's history; the manuscript of Muslim notable Abu al-Su'ud al-Hasibi and other studies ascribe the violence to accumulated frustrations of the city's Muslim working and rural elements at a changing economic order that they associated with Europe, and they took vengeance on their perceived local beneficiaries, the Christians.[1] In a forceful response by the government in Istanbul to preclude French interference on the part of local Christians, the old order of Muslim notability was cleared away, and reform-minded statesmen found the province of Damascus a canvas on which to test and prove their reform (Tanzimat) philosophy. Not only Fuad Pasha, the Ottoman foreign minister and lead reformer, but also his more able successors in Damascus implemented stark new reforms as a means of controlling and disciplining the unruly city. Their actions resulted in the creation of new forms of public order, public space, and the public sphere—reshaping the Damascene environment with the intent of making it more docile and homogenous. In investing the political capital of the reform movement in Damascus, they sowed the seeds of a new sense of Damascene sovereignty, which may have made the city ultimately more difficult to tie to Istanbul.

Twenty years earlier, in 1840, the Ottomans with the help of the British had dislodged from Syria Ibrahim Pasha, the son of Egypt's Muhammad 'Ali. Muhammad 'Ali's rule in Egypt and invasion and occupation of the key Ottoman regions of the Eastern Mediterranean were lessons in the necessity of reform. The renegade Ottoman military officer cemented his hold on the province of Egypt through Westernizing changes to the military and the economy.[2] His success was testimony to the importance of reform. That his progress could only be held back with European assistance was testimony to Ottoman decline. In the 1840s and 1850s, European influence in the Arabic-speaking provinces increased in the form of missionary schools and heightened trade. The restitution of order after 1860 was a chance for Istanbul to reassert itself. The most effective Ottoman governors were those who, armed with visions of a reformed, orderly, and taxable province, invested in campaigns of public order, the creation of a public sphere, and public infrastructure.

Traditional Ottoman provincial policy was based on preventing upstart provincial notables from becoming too strong and on rotating Ottoman officeholders to prevent them from building up power bases in provincial centers that might become too independent of the center.[3] The Ottoman overextension of the eighteenth century and the eruptions of unruly provincial centers and rebellious pashas throughout the Arab provinces were situations to be avoided. In the nineteenth century, the Sublime Porte in Istanbul had more technologies, techniques, and resources with which to control secondary centers like Damascus. Mastery of technologies, techniques, and resources of control emanating from the imperial center, however, gave Ottoman men of vision new political capital, and several of Damascus's more visionary governors of the second half of the long nineteenth century were able to practice new styles of government that began to transform Damascus into a city with a distinct new identity, even as they attempted to integrate it more fully and docilely into a new Ottoman order.[4] It was these governors who made the changes of modernity stick in a place like Damascus. They had access to this political capital from Istanbul and the opportunity to exercise it in Damascus in ways impossible in the metropole, and they did so as part of consolidation of their own political, military, or administrative careers.

In the context discussed here—that of Ottoman governors of Damascus—political capital consists of two elements, one coming from Istanbul and the other related to political maneuvering in Damascus. On the one hand, political capital consisted of legitimate authority from the Sultan and central government (and secondarily, the latitude and financial resources to use that authority free from disabling rivalries or other limitations). On the other hand, in Damascus, political capital consisted of the ability to use (or override) the local power structure, the system of local notability, personalities, and sources of wealth to effect change. The fact that investment in infrastructure and reform suited the needs and desires of Istanbul and old Damascus allowed powerful actors to change the city dramatically. As with family, demography, and religious knowledge, this form of cultural capital I call political capital is a nebulous thing, not easily reducible to economic terms by any means.

In this chapter, I will discuss the strategies, policies, and visions of modernist Ottoman governors that were translated into the growth and transformation of Damascus. The effect of these changes was the creation of publicness—the formation of public spaces and façades, public transportation and schools, public companies, a public sphere in the sense of journalism and associations, and an intense concern with public safety that had the goal of subduing and dominating the unruly fringes of Damascus society. The enduring evidence of this transformation can be seen in the city's public buildings, spaces, and institutions.

If there was a period that might be labeled a period of transition to architectural modernity, it was between the 1870s and 1908, coincident with late Ottoman reform projects. This was the period in which the Ottoman governors of Damascus sponsored and encouraged a number of public works projects in which emphasis was placed on changing forms, functions, and façades befitting a provincial capital. This was the period of monumental and ornately façaded structures standing alone in space, asserting their difference from the modest exteriors and hidden interiors and courtyards nested in the Islamic city. In this period, Marjah Square just west of and outside the walls of the city became the center as new public buildings clustered there. Between the 1870s and 1908, more public buildings were erected along the avenues defined by the Barada River. Along with rebuilding the public face of the city, the political capital of various governments was also applied to reorganizing the population, the relations between the city and various parts of its rural hinterlands, and the function of provincial administration.[5]

Over the course of the nineteenth century, major infrastructural and administrative development in the province of Damascus took place in a top-down fashion at the initiative of its governors. The urban and administrative legacies of the terms of Fuad Pasha (1860–1866), Rashid Pasha

(1866–1871), Midhat Pasha (1878–1880), and Nazim Pasha (1897–1909; see chapter 7)—whose tenures were interspersed with successions of weak and forgettable governors—are the foundation of twentieth-century Syria and foreshadowed the military rule of Jamal Pasha during World War I. Fuad Pasha established order against the local *'ulama,* weak bureaucrats, and European interventionism. Mehmet Rashid Pasha extended communications networks and put into place a new subsystem of local rule. Midhat Pasha used Syria as a base for empirewide administrative reform. What distinguishes these strong governors from the forgettable rulers of the 1840s, 1850s, 1870s, and 1880s was their ability to use their strength not to establish entirely autocratic rule but to coordinate Ottoman reform policy and local needs and dramatically change the structure of the city.[6] Rather than being mere functionaries, they were "dangerous" individuals who, exiled or dispatched away from Istanbul for political reasons, turned a provincial post into a testing ground for their more ambitious cosmopolitan visions.

The three reforming governors discussed in this chapter—Fuad, Mehmed Rashid, and Midhat—were particularly skilled at melding and using these two forms of political capital: authority brought to Damascus with them from Istanbul and the ability to use the particular local system of Damascus to get things done. The effective use of authority from the central power and good management of local agents and resources resulted in the ability to change a landscape like that of Damascus. The changes concerned security, communications, and transportation infrastructure, as well as administrative units. Also, the face of the city was changed by the use of these different kinds of political capital. In this period, the city acquired European-style public spaces, façades, and public services and became connected by telegraph, roads, and railroads to other cities. More importantly, it developed a new territorial and social integrity as the new province of Suriyya.

Fuad Pasha and Public Safety (1860–1866): Asserting the Ottoman Order

The period between 1860, in the wake of the Christian massacres, and 1865, when his protégé Rushdi Pasha was replaced as governor of Syria, was marked by Ottoman foreign minister and later grand vizier Fuad Pasha's influence in Syria. A British observer summed up the romantic European view of Fuad Pasha and his place as a force and a symbol of the liberal view of the Ottoman reawakening, calling him "a man of modern ideas whose influence pervades every department of the Government."[7] Fuad articulated his own vision of Ottoman reform in what became known as the testament of 1869 when he called for radical changes in all political and civil institutions, based on an open and expansive Islam but emphasizing total equality for all groups; separation of state from religion; unity; and a reformed judiciary, educational system, and transportation infrastructure. These principles had been applied a decade earlier in Damascus under his military rule.

In 1860, Fuad personally imposed a stern punitive regime in Damascus, marking the end of outright control by the urban notables and the beginning of more effective Ottoman authority. Because the issue of the 1860 upheaval was an international affair, it was logical that Fuad's virtually unbounded local control was augmented by his powers as the foreign minister. When he was recalled to Istanbul in 1861 to become grand vizier, it was because he had proven himself to be the best reconciler of provincial and international strategy. His influence while in the province and in Istanbul is best understood in terms of the creation of public order. He purged the local Muslim power structure that had allowed the massacres to occur. He used a conscripted army locally to reign in the Bedouin, deployed new weapons technology and surveillance techniques to keep them subdued, and settled them. Under martial law, the Fifth Army Corps pushed back the Bedouin, Druze, and outlaws of the province and enlisted the manpower of the province in a conscripted army. He used his position in Istanbul to finance and establish a Syrian gendarmerie.[8] This period, begun in sectarian urban violence, ended with the tentative administrative unification of the Syrian province.

Fuad arrived in Damascus on July 29, 1860, to scenes of general chaos. As special commissioner to Syria with full military and civil powers and a force of fifteen thousand men, his mission was to restore the credibility of the Ottoman government in the aftermath of the Christian massacres.[9] His first job consisted of punishing those responsible for the brutality at all levels and forestalling the further incursions of France on the pretext of protecting the Syrian Christians. To the power of special commissioner to Damascus was added shortly thereafter the powers of the Ottoman foreign minister. In the first week of August, eight hundred people were arrested, starting with the ordinary Muslims of the working and criminal classes. Tribunals, executions, and exiles continued throughout August and September. On October 19, the members of the advisory council, the main local consultative body dominated by Muslim notables, were sent into exile. On September 7, after some hesitation, Ahmad Pasha, the governor of Damascus, was executed along with other high-ranking Ottoman officers who had failed to prevent the killings. In the winter of 1861, after the period of punishment, steps were taken to provide housing, goods, and money for the Christians, and reparatory taxes were levied on Muslim and Jewish Damascenes.[10]

Fuad's second job was to subdue the more unruly groups around Damascus. The policy of Bedouin surveillance and Druze control, an important part of Fuad's legacy in Syria, was based on the new ability of the Ottoman army to conscript urban Syrians into the Fifth Army Corps. The process of conscription or drafting a citizen army and using it locally for inroads against the Bedouin tribes in the campaign of 1863 was a pillar of his new policy. Up to 10 percent of the male population between the ages of eighteen and twenty-five provided ten thousand men to the Fifth Army Corps. Rather than being transferred to a distant part of the empire, they were trained locally and stationed in Syria. This locally manned fighting force was much more effective in countering the Bedouin and other unruly elements than one composed of recruits from distant parts of the empire. In 1863, a reserve component of the Fifth Army Corps was created and nearly all the able-bodied men in Syria had some connection with the army. At the end of 1863 and into 1864, an inspection team from Istanbul worked in Damascus to refine the Fifth Army Corps. Its finances were investigated, salary arrears were paid, barracks were renovated and expanded, the hospital sanitized, new uniforms ordered, and modern training and drilling techniques put into practice. With the new and improved army in place, martial law was terminated in 1864.[11]

Bedouin mobility and predation on agricultural settlements was, in the view of many observers, the primary factor in unsettling the countryside and thereby allowing criminal elements and rebellious communities like the Druze to flourish. For Fuad and the commandants who ruled the province under martial law, dealing with the Bedouin meant restoring a line of demarcation in cooperation with other provincial governors between the agricultural areas of the Fertile Crescent and the desert, a line marked by fortresses along the western bank of the Euphrates to the Persian Gulf. The campaign against the Bedouin in 1863 consisted of refortifying the defense line between Syria and the desert. Surveillance of Bedouin movements was also part of the new policy. Barracks were constructed at regular intervals of the frontier line. Some soldiers kept watch while other troops moved to bar Bedouin incursions into settled territory.[12] The other decisive aspect of the campaign of 1863 by Mushir Halim Pasha against the Bedouin tribes was that the Fifth Army Corps had acquired breach-loading repeating rifles and other modern firearms in the Crimean War. With this superior weaponry, they were able to more effectively pursue the nomads and confiscate their herds and flocks for sale in Damascus markets to finance the campaigns. Even the larger tribal confederations that united from time to time in the early 1860s were unable to counter the Ottoman forces. In October of 1863, the governor of Damascus was approached by a representative of the tribes requesting safe passage to towns and villages for the purchase of grain for the winter.[13]

The next security issue with which Fuad Pasha and his lieutenants had to deal was the issue of the Druze community. The Druze of Mt. Lebanon had initiated the civil war with that region's Christians, and the Druze of the Hawran had been a major element in the riots and massacres of 1860 in Damascus itself. European governments (particularly France, the traditional defender of Syrian Christians) were adamant that the Druze should be punished. In September of 1860, a French and Ottoman military campaign to Mt. Lebanon drove thousands of Druze fugitives to the Jabal Druze area in the Hawran. Until amnesty was granted to them in 1865, they posed a constant threat to the Ottoman order. Because of international pressure, Fuad was not able to compromise or make conciliatory efforts toward this disruptive element. The question was therefore one of enforcing security by means of strength. Mounting a military expedition against the Hawran and the Druze had proved disastrous at least twice before for Ibrahim Pasha and an Ottoman governor in 1852. When attacked, the Druze went into hiding in the rocky plains of the Laja' where they raided the other agriculturalists of the Hawran for food and to put pressure on the government. During Fuad's period of martial law, their demand was amnesty from the sentences resulting from the events of 1860.

The government response to this situation was to surround the Laja' with army outposts without actually attacking the Druze and to focus on disabling the more vulnerable of their allies—the Bedouins and the brigands. By 1863, when the Bedouin problem was solved, and 1864, when many of the bands of highwaymen had been rounded up by the army and gendarmerie, the Druze were deprived of their support and were forced into negotiations with the government. The Druze leaders sent their sons to negotiate for them in Damascus; in return for paying outstanding taxes, paying a military exemption tax, and turning in outlaws, it seemed they might earn their amnesty from the Sultan. By August 1865, the Druze were paying the annual 240,000-piaster military exemption tax by loads of grain sent to Damascus. In addition, the Druze accepted the positioning of an Ottoman administrator or *mudir* in their Jabal Druze stronghold.[14]

The net effect of Fuad's public-order campaigns was to bring heretofore unruly groups more or less under the control of the government using new technologies and cumulative tactics.

Rushdi Pasha's Governorship:
An *'Alim* and the New Province

While in Beirut and Damascus, Fuad had also undertaken administrative reform of Mt. Lebanon, introduced a telegraph connection between Damascus and Istanbul, and assigned the concession for the Beirut-Damascus road that would tie Damascus to the coast. This public-development work in the civil realm was continued by his handpicked governor for Damascus. Rushdi Pasha, whom Fuad appointed governor of Damascus after his own recall to Istanbul, was a member of the Istanbul *'ulama*. He knew Arabic, and his ability to consult with and placate the Damascus *'ulama* was helpful in restoring normalcy after the humiliation of the upper echelons of the *'ulama* in the aftermath of the upheavals of 1860. In the spring of 1864, with the end of martial law, he immediately prepared to reconstruct the Christian quarter of Damascus, which had been largely destroyed in the 1860 disturbances. Under Rushdi Pasha, the streets of Damascus were widened so that wheeled vehicles arriving from the coast by means of the new Beirut-Damascus carriage road could enter the city. Swamp drainage on the outskirts of the Ghuta was another major project, and under Rushdi's leadership these works seem to have been carried out in an efficient manner. The foreign consuls exclaimed that the workers were being paid full wages on time. A *majlis al-baladiyya* or municipal council comprising notables from the different religious communities of Damascus was set up and given "authority to levy rates for lighting, paving, cleansing and guarding the city. . . . and public improvements."[15] As a result of these improvements and of Fuad Pasha's continuing interest in Syrian affairs, commerce revived in the years of Rushdi Pasha's governorship.[16] Foreign missionary activity recommenced after an abrupt stop in 1860, and European tourism began to be a more common phenomenon.

In 1865, the Ottoman Law of the *Wilayat* (provinces)—designed to apply the Tanzimat reforms to provincial government and to subject the provinces to the rule of law rather than the rule of men—was tried out in Syria a few weeks after its primary test case in the Danube Province of the Balkans. Rushdi Pasha was to become the new governor of *wilayat* Suriyya, created by the union of Damascus and Sidon provinces. But it was also a means of consolidating the newly important link of the interior with the coast (rather than Arabia). Beirut and Damascus both underwent this transition, and the governor oversaw the entire new province, which was defined as a multicity territory of coast and interior.[17]

The end of the period of Fuad Pasha's influence in Syria was marked by an outbreak of cholera in the new province of Suriyya in 1865. Rushdi Pasha, like the rest of the elite, left for the Anti-Lebanon Mountains both to escape the cholera and oversee administrative reform outside of the capital. He then proceeded to Hamah, Hums, Tripoli, and Beirut, where word came by telegraph of his replacement as governor.[18] Ironically, wherever he went, the cholera followed, emphasizing in a perverse way the unity of the new province in which population had begun to grow and travel had been made so much easier than in the past. The cholera that swept from city to city highlighted the need for continued reform beyond the skills of army commanders and *'ulama.*

Mehmed Rashid Pasha and the Public Sphere (1866–1871): Building the Province of Suriyya

Mehmed Rashid Pasha came to power in Syria in 1866 as a result of the change of government in Istanbul, which replaced Fuad Pasha with 'Ali Pasha as the grand vizier. He is remembered by Syrian historians as strongest and best *wali* of Syria, and his governorship was characterized by a sense of modernization and progress. During the five years of his rule, Suriyya the province was effectively created by expansion of communications and transportation, continuation of administrative and judicial reform, and military subduing of the rebellious elements of the province. After ending his work in Syria, Rashid went on to become Minister of Public Works in Istanbul and was mistakenly killed by an assassin's bullet in 1876.

Rashid Pasha's father had been in the service of Muhammad 'Ali. He himself was thus born and raised in Egypt. Later he studied in Paris, and his fluency in both French and Arabic was key to his advancement. As a modernist, he was preoccupied with contemporary forms of art and literature. It was during Rashid Pasha's governorship of Syria that the *nahda* or Arabic literary renaissance is said to have begun. He had a personal interest in spreading literacy and in the building of an educational infrastructure.[19] With his encouragement, primary schools were established in Damascus, Beirut, and Jerusalem. A provincial newspaper, *Suriyya,* began to circulate, and periodical *salnamas* (yearbooks) for the province began to be produced. In this atmosphere of reading and writing, private literary journals also began to be produced.[20]

Communication and transportation infrastructure, first installed under Fuad Pasha's influence, continued to be expanded in Rashid Pasha's governorate. Telegraphy facilities spread to every important town of the province, and European languages as well as Turkish could be transmitted. Husni says of Rashid Pasha that he was in love with the telegraph and spent hours on end in the telegraph office sending and receiving messages.[21] Rashid also initiated an important campaign of road and bridge building. He recommended and oversaw the building of carriage roads between Damascus and Palestine that facilitated Egyptian trade, and a road north to Ma'arra and on to Majdal-'Anjar. Other road projects initiated in his governorship joined inland cities to the coast—Homs and Tripoli, Sidon and Nablus, Tyre and Tabnina, Acre and Suq al-Khan—as well as easing the connections between inland cities (Nablus and Jerusalem) and coastal cities (Beirut and Sidon, Jaffa and Gaza).[22] He intended to resurrect the defunct Damascus-to-Baghdad commercial route, but this ambitious plan was not brought to fruition.

Rashid's program of enforcing the new provincial law included recommending the establishment of commercial courts, commercial banks, uniform weights and measures, and a campaign promoting Syrian goods in Istanbul. He promoted the idea of establishing an agricultural *majlis* (council) in each town, government provision of planting seed to peasants for the cultivation of new or abandoned land, and initially the settlement of Bedouin tribes though grants of free seed from the government. It is unknown whether he achieved his plans for promoting industry and organization of workers into groups resembling guilds. He was an early proponent of local tax reform and Arabic language law codes in the province. In accordance with the new Law of the *Wilayat*, Rashid Pasha convened the first Syrian parliament. Four delegates from each administrative district, two Muslims and two non-Muslims, discussed matters relating to commerce, infrastructures, and administration starting on December 1, 1867, in Beirut.[23]

Subduing Bedouins and Druze continued to be crucial to a successful gubernatorial tenure in Suriyya province, and Rashid distinguished himself militarily. In subduing Jabal al-Nusayriyya, Jabal Druze, and the Bedouins, he built on the public security envisioned by Fuad Pasha and contributed to the stability of the newly united Suriyya province. It was his belief, and one he acted on, that a formidable military policy was the sine qua non for the infrastructural, educational, and administrative reforms that he felt so strongly about. One of his first actions as governor in 1866 was to carry out the executions of some bandits. As with Fuad Pasha, the authorization to put locals to death caught the attention of the Syrians.[24] Rashid's Bedouin policy involved coordination with the governor of neighboring Aleppo province by telegraph, and telegraph communication between the surveillance outposts.[25] Capitalizing on the success, in 1867 he was able to compel both the Druze and the northern Bedouin into service for a campaign against the southern Bedouin. The expedition met only weak resistance from most of the tribes and quickly received their submission and approximately 4 million piasters of taxes in livestock and grain.[26] In 1869, he returned to the region at the head of another expedition to enforce the resettlement of the Banu Sakhr tribe from lands that had been sold by the state under the new land law regime and to prevent the recalcitrant tribe from taking revenge on the returning hajj caravan. As before, he enlisted the aid of Druze and northern Bedouin to intimidate the southern tribes. He received their submission and set the precedent of making the surrendered tribe pay for the costs of the expedition.[27]

In a sign of the times and the increasing autonomy of the new province of Suriyya under its strong ruler, Rashid Pasha's enemy was the British consul Richard Burton, who served in Damascus from 1868 to 1870 and whose reports of the *wali*'s actions make him out to be a tyrant. According to his own superiors in the British Foreign Office, Burton deeply resented the shift in powers between the European consuls and the provincial governor.[28] Ottoman reform in Damascus was curtailing the considerable power of the European consuls.

Rashid's success in his military campaigns against the southern tribes allowed him to gain complete executive power over appointments in his province.[29] This new power allowed him to institute a patterned series of appointments that integrated local with imperial district subheads. In the relatively calm and flourishing coastal districts of Beirut, Tripoli, and Acre, he positioned Turkish officials. In the more troublesome districts of the interior—Hamah, Hawran, and also Nablus (the headquarters of his campaigns against of the southern tribes)—and as commander of the hajj pilgrimage caravan, he appointed local Kurdish strongmen whose families would be among the most influential notables of the last years of the century.

Like Fuad, Rashid emphasized security, administrative reform, and technology of communication and transportation, and in doing so he consolidated the new province of Suriyya, which extended from the coast into the interior. Like Fuad, he was adept at using lieutenants and intermediaries to maximize his influence.

Midhat Pasha's Rule (1878–1880):
Province as Blueprint for Empire

If the period of Fuad Pasha's influence began the transformation of the interior Damascus province into the coastal Suriyya province, and Rashid Pasha's rule marked the successful consolidation of Suriyya province through the mobilization of local culture and leaders, Midhat Pasha's ambitions sketched the broader and less successful attempt to make centralized provincial rule the very basis of the empire. His reform attempts in the province of Suriyya have been understood as a blueprint for the empirewide reform he hoped to effect when back in full power in Istanbul. His presence in Syria as an exile, in the waning years of his career, in continuous tension with the Sultan, thwarted most of his attempts at reform. Where his partner in the creation of the Law of the Wilayat, Fuad, had enjoyed unlimited powers of reform in 1860 and 1861, Midhat's equally far-reaching vision of provincial order threatened the despotic tendencies of Sultan 'Abdulhamid. Midhat's insistence on more executive power and the growing anti-Ottoman popular agitation during his rule caused him to be nicknamed the *khedive* of Syria, echoing the independence of the dynasty of Muhammad 'Ali.

Having failed in his project of constitutional promulgation at the highest level of Ottoman government and having spent several months in Europe and Crete in exile, Midhat was nominated as governor general of Syria in October 1878 at the behest of the British ambassador.[30] Strictly limited provincial government was the traditional place for an experienced yet dangerous reformer like Midhat. Evidently optimistic about the imminent fall of 'Abdulhamid, Midhat prepared a detailed memorandum on necessary reforms in the government of Syria.[31] At the center of the *Suriye Layihasi,* as the reform proposal was titled, was more power for the governor based on the claim that Syria in particular was subject to chaos resulting from complex social forces and European pressure. He called for a return to the provisions of the Law of the Wilayat, emergency funding to fill vacant posts, the return of Damascus's status to a *mutassariflik* separate from its hinterland, and the governor's right to assign and pay reasonable salaries. He insisted on the right to personally appoint all his subordinates in the province— *mutassarifs, qai'maqams,* and judges. Hampered by local corruption and by halfhearted cooperation of the Porte in fighting it, Midhat attempted to curb the corruption of the Syrian councils and judiciary by calling for higher salaries, for his personal right to supervise council elections, and for his right to oversee the entire judiciary system of the province. Not surprisingly, most of his proposals were refused by the Porte.[32]

Midhat Pasha's greatest successes as an administrator were in the area of economic reform—no mean feat after the war, poor harvests, depressions, and financial crises of the 1870s. In fiscal matters, he was more successful in proving his point about local control and autonomy. Spurred on by specific British demands for fiscal reform and his own ideas about the rationalization of revenue generation, he proposed to abolish the *iltizam* (tax farm) system once and for all and replace it with a land tax and poll tax similar to the system of the Règlement Organique in Lebanon.[33] Unable to effect such a far-reaching change without the full support of the central government, which only supplied him with a new tax collecting office and the vague promise of change, he used his influence to change the system by which *iltizams* were auctioned off. In the bidding process of 1879, Midhat intervened to enforce public and open bidding on the right to collect taxes from individual villages rather than entire districts, and the new possibility of communal bidding by the inhabitants of a village with payment delayed until the harvest. That season, a full 30 percent increase in the revenues of 75,000 Turkish pounds (TL) was realized.[34]

Midhat also had radical ideas about how funds should be allocated. Most startling was his suggestion that the Syrian-sponsored hajj caravan and the 100,000 TL spent on it each year should be abolished. Midhat suggested that the province of Aleppo should pay half of the burden of supporting the Fifth Army Corps. This reallocation of revenue, Midhat argued, would free 100,000 TL (three times more than the existing allotment) to pay government salaries and thus prevent corruption, and an additional 125,000 TL for public works projects. This was a dramatic reordering of priorities and would still provide 400,000 TL in tax revenues for Istanbul.[35]

Realistic about the need for foreign capital for railway schemes, Midhat focused on road building suited to the local economy: the extension of the Homs-Tripoli road to Damascus and Lataqia, an offshoot of the Damascus-Beirut carriage road to Shtura and B'aalbeck, and projects for roads from Lataqia to Jisr in Aleppo province and between Lataqia and Hama. He was working on plans for a road from Damascus to Nabatiyya and Sidon when he was ultimately removed from office.

His contribution to the city of Damascus, along with the broad covered market that bears his name to this day, was a carriage road from Damascus up to al-Salihiyya and carriage roads along the banks of the Barada River. For several of these projects, he used forced labor when support was unavailable either from Istanbul or provincial sources. The emphasis in all his road projects was on facilitating commerce within Syria, consolidating Ottoman political and military control, and connecting the inland with the ports.[36]

Midhat contracted with an English engineer to carry out feasibility studies for a railroad from the Euphrates to Tripoli, modern harbor facilities in the coastal towns, and a railroad across the Anti-Lebanon Mountains connecting Beirut and Damascus (an idea deemed impracticable). Serious railbuilding projects in Syria, however, were still two decades away. Tramways were more affordable, and a 3-kilometer line from the center of Tripoli to the port was completed in February 1880. Midhat again proved himself to be a creative financier in the absence of funds from Istanbul; he seems to have organized a company with British and local capital amounting to 8,000 TL, of which he himself invested 200.[37]

Midhat Pasha's vision of the new Syria called for networks of communication and more systematic public education. In a continuation of the progress made in Rashid Pasha's day, the telegraph system was extended and improved, as was the postal system. In the two years of Midhat's rule, he paid a great deal of attention to educational issues. Among the thirty new schools opened throughout the province were a girls' school, an industrial arts school, and an orphanage. Although there were several new state-supported *rushdiyya* or secondary schools, most of the schools were supported by charitable organizations of Muslim notables encouraged by Midhat to counter the head start of the foreign missionary schools in Syria since the 1840s and flourishing again since the 1860s. During Midhat's governorship, more than a dozen newspapers were published in various cities of the province. It was Midhat who encouraged the 'alim Tahir al-Jaza'iri to establish the Zahiriyya Library.[38]

Subduing the semiautonomous and chronically rebellious groups living in the mountains and deserts was a corollary to strengthening the executive control of the *wali*. Midhat was an ardent proponent of settling the Bedouin in order to control them and also to generate revenue from increasing the amount of cultivated land. He was in favor of a strong and modern army and police force and had no qualms about using them to keep the Bedouin and other privileged communities like the Druze of the Hawran and the inhabitants of Jabal al-Nusayriyya in line. He proposed further increasing revenue through the curtailing of the privileges of highland populations, protection of agriculturalists from usury of various sorts, controlled resettlement of unproductive lands, and regulation of land registration and tax collection. Yet here again he was stymied by lack of authorization from Istanbul and the tenacity of local notables who found the status quo quite lucrative.[39]

In the second year of his tenure as governor of Syria, Midhat simply was inactive. He went on a long vacation to Beirut after an ineffective attempt to quell the Druze and his attempt at resignation. He left provincial affairs to the *mutassarifs* and *qa'imaqams* and forwarded most policy question to Istanbul for decision. It has been suggested that his inertia was a means of prolonging his stay in Syria in light of the inhospitable political climate of Istanbul. The inactivity definitely contributed to his unpopularity among the people of Syria. In October 1879, he was denounced publicly by a shaykh of the Ummayad Mosque in Damascus, and as usual, used the resulting chaos to argue for an augmentation of the governor's jurisdiction. His opponents used these troubles to argue for his dismissal. In June of 1880, placards calling upon the inhabitants of Syria to revolt against Ottoman rule appeared in Beirut, and they appeared during the next weeks in Damascus and other towns. Observers conjectured that Midhat himself might have been behind his own opposition movement, so relaxed was he as to finding and punishing the placards' authors. His opponents spread rumors that Midhat, with British support, sought Syria's secession from the Empire and called him, after Muhammad 'Ali, the "*Khedive* of Syria."[40]

When the conservative government of Disraeli fell in the spring of 1880 and was replaced by the liberal and anti-Ottoman government of Gladstone, Midhat again tendered his resignation, indicating by deed, if not by explicit word, that his role in Syria was more closely related to international affairs than provincial ones. The Sultan again refused to accept his resignation, and the return of the reformist party to power in Istanbul in June 1880 encouraged his belief that his return to higher office in the capital was imminent. On the contrary, in the next weeks the Sultan once again turned against Midhat, perhaps viewing him as a serious rival. When Midhat was recalled in August 1880, it was to the governorate of Izmir, not the post of grand vizier. This was the beginning of the end of his career.

Nevertheless, his emphasis on strong governorship left its mark on local life and psyche. It was not his liberal program, rather his overriding concern with provincial self-sufficiency and executive power—which combined the waywardness of a *khedive*, the apparently liberal reformism of Fuad, and the local pragmatism of Rashid—that made Midhat Pasha the best-remembered governor of nineteenth-century Syria. Each of these three governors disciplined the *Sham* (Damascene system) by spending political capital on radical reforms. Fuad punished and dismantled the old system, which had allowed the 1860 massacres to occur, and began reconstruction in a liberal mold. Rashid subdued the unruly outlying elements of the system and encouraged the local sense of cultural coherence. Midhat's greatest contribution was to economic self-sufficiency and reform that would allow the new province to stand alone as a semi-autonomous unit. The later "mandate," which crudely embodied a notion of an immature society under the tutelage of a foreign regime of governance, was applied to a system that had just undergone its own unique process of development.

Under the rules of reforming Ottoman governors, the new province of Suriyya developed into the prototype of a nation-state. Fuad, Rashid, and Midhat manipulated the imperial legitimacy they brought with them from the Porte, and their ability to translate it into public order, public spheres, and public space effected a reshaping of the space of al-Sham in which the government had more at stake than ever before in the commons areas of city and society.

The stronger governors of Damascus of the second half of the long nineteenth century were able to envision and apply a very real program of administrative reform, infrastructural growth, and even political modernism. The indicators of this trend were an increasingly extensive and elaborate system of roads, railway projects, and telegraph links and the development of the city of Damascus into a city of Western-style façades, public spaces, monuments, and boulevards. Through both the reform period and the autocratic Hamidian period, however, there were constant pressures, a continuous need for more resources of various kinds. Larger projects required greater financial investment and required new sources of capital, even as local tax resources were exhausted, and successful rule required rationalization of provincial finances. A last form of capital was also required in the form of support in Istanbul. A governor's hands could easily be tied by imperial hostility or even indifference. Midhat's rule in Syria ended in failure because of his precarious and ambiguous relations with 'Abdulhamid.

The intent of the Tanzimat reforms forcefully impressed on Suriyya between 1860 and 1880 was to control the province's populace more effectively for the individual governors and for the benefit of the empire. Instead, it created public environments, a sense of population, and an interest in the provincial collective self.

If the practices of the successful governors started as the imposition of order so that liberal ideals could flourish, the response of the governed was to make liberal use of the new space for expression in order to envision autonomy.[41] When the telegraph linking the garrisons of the Damascus area to Istanbul was set up, for example, it did not just work one way. The British consul remembered, "A great interest in telegraphic appeal to the Sultan of nearly all junior officers stationed here for the payment of arrears pay due to them"[42] (which were duly paid).

New forms of protest were suggested by the new technologies and their implications for traditional ways of life. For Rashid Pasha, countless hours in the telegraph office could not easily resolve the problem of how to keep the telegraph poles standing, since "the Bedouin tribes beyond Ma'an are constantly pulling down and carrying off the telegraph poles of the new line as fast as they are put up. It would appear that the insulators in particular are exciting mingled feelings of curiosity and terror in the breasts on the ground and that they are, so they believe, the chosen home and abode of the 'jinn,'" in the words of a later British consul.[43]

Likewise, the interest of the government in harnessing its new citizenry for conscription in the army and the enhancement of provincial security resulted in the migration of thousands of young Syrian men out of their villages and towns, into the anonymity of Levantine city life, and on to opportunities of citizenship in the new world. Estimates by European consuls of deserters from Suriyya put the number at nineteen thousand by the end of the century, almost half of the total imperial desertions.[44]

Moving on from the capital-intensive actions of the powerful to those of ordinary people which are harder to document but no less important cumulatively, the next four chapters use the resources of the *shari'a* court archives to investigate trends in the Sunni Muslim population of Damascus after 1880.[45]

3

BAB AL-WATHA'IQ:
ON ARCHIVAL CAPITAL

An invaluable window on the ordinary people of Damascus, whose activities profoundly shaped the city's cultural topography, is what I shall call "archival capital." This chapter has two objectives. It first describes the archives—in this case primarily the probate inventories (*mukhallafat* or *tarikat*) of the inheritance division (*qassam*) of the Islamic law courts of Damascus—and discusses their analytical utility. Second, through a quantitative survey, it reveals some tantalizing indications of cultural secularization, urban modernization, and the changing relationship of the citizen to the state. These indications serve as a prologue to the more detailed discussion of mercantile, human, intellectual, and political capital to follow in subsequent chapters.

Datamining: Discerning Patterns of Change
The survey of probate inventories provides quantifiable data allowing the comparison of individuals and groups vis-à-vis the everyday practices of naming, family building, financial matters, consumption, and style. Trends in the practice of naming can be identified—the relative power of conservatism versus innovation. Relationships between an individual and his family, the practices of family building, and channeling of resources to family are clarified. The practices of wealth accumulation and how they changed over time become evident.

The other type of information that inheritance records supply is also useful. That, of course, is data on what people owned. This gives not only a basis for comparison and the understanding of wealth differentials, but concrete information about how wealth was built, stored, and transferred. This data about what people owned and of what their fortunes consisted is a primary source on cultural capital circulating in the city under study. My daily sorting through the archives and noting variables of inheritance documents was a basic form of what we today call datamining. This means combing large stores of data for patterns or the "nontrivial extraction of implicit, previously unknown, and potentially useful information from data."[1] My approach was to examine the *shari'a* court archives not for individual narratives, which are all but invisible in the highly structured format, but rather for impressions of a changing city through the accumulation of individual choices. How people are named, how their status is represented, where they live, and their relationship to the state are visible as trends over the population of estates divided. We see a society changing, being reshaped by the small and otherwise unrecorded choices about personal lives. Moreover, we see the changes we associate with modernity.

The data from the probate inventories reveal no dramatic watershed events but rather a continuous, gradual, cumulative process of change. World War I, a traumatic event for the province of Damascus, leaves little in the way of traces other than an upsurge in the number of cases in which two probate processes within the same household are recorded in a single case or in successive cases—family members dying during the same period of time as a result of disease or hunger. Without knowing any of the context or structures of the city, one can nevertheless document a gradual transformation in less visible ways. My own initial transcriptions of the variable information in the formal inheritance documents showed that people's naming practices were changing, residential patterns were changing, and use of status titles was changing. In addition, changes in the composition of the registers themselves revealed the encroachment of the Ottoman provincial state on the realm of the Islamic courts.

A source of difficulty was that birth dates and ages of the deceased were not given in the documents, and the relationship between the date of death and the date of probate was not clear. To get a sample of reasonable size given this imprecision, I collected data about people whose estates were recorded between 1300 and 1310 (AH)—roughly 1880 to 1890—on the assumption that their possessions would have been acquired during the decades prior to their death. For comparison, I collected data from the last decade of available court records, 1330–1340 AH (roughly 1910–1920). Comparisons would provide information about broad and wide changes in the last decades of the century without enabling more specific dating.

The Probate Inventories (*al-Mukhallafat*)

The inheritance records or probate inventories (*mukhallafat* or *tarikat,* literally "the things left behind") are highly formal court documents. Moreover, there are inheritance records for people of poor, middling, and wealthy means, both men and women, within the Sunni Muslim community. The painstaking gleaning of patterns from them provides insight not only into what people owned, but into how property relations shaped the Damascus family and how wealth accumulation helped shape the city itself.

Through the probate inventory, the individual appears as the nexus of highly structured relations of kinship and ownership. The accidents of particularity that position that person at a specific point or location in the social matrix are made clear. And some of the choices and expressions of personality that suggest the life lived in all its social and emotional complexity are just barely suggested. But the examination of a series of documents of a type produced by the *shari'a* system illustrates the formal patterns of how wealth devolves from generation to generation. It also illustrates the emerging differences in wealth between rich and poor and between men and women. The consideration of these documents suggests the metaphor of liquid sloshing through the distribution channels of the society. The tracks of wealth are too complex, numerous, and minute to follow, and each document is presented without context. There is no continuity of documentation or easy cross-referencing to other documents, such as sales contracts or marriage agreements. But the probate inventories show how the resources of the society tended to pool and stagnate as they were appropriated by owners.

I used the probate inventories registered in the Damascus *qassam* (inheritance specialists, literally "divider") courts between 1880 and 1920, the last forty years covered by the registers in the *Markaz lil Watha'iq al-Tarikhiyya* in Suq Saruja in Damascus. One of the main branches of Islamic law that developed a special branch of the courts was *qisma* (literally "division") or probate. The probate judge (*qassam*) evaluated and distributed the estates of deceased persons according to Islamic law of inheritance (*'ilm al-fara'id*) among their survivors and inheritors.[2] For most of the Ottoman period, there were two *qassams*. The *qassam 'arabi* or *qassam baladi* handled the estates of local residents while the *qassam 'askari* dealt with the estates of the Ottoman military and officialdom, although by the end of the nineteenth century and early twentieth century the two seem to have merged.[3] Of the approximately 800 registers of court cases, approximately a few dozen contain only the probate inventories evaluated by the *qassam.* I focused on the last cataloged *sijills* (registers) of *tarikat* available in the Damascus *shari'a* court archives as the most likely location for dramatic evidence of a transformation in the lives of ordinary people. I surveyed the six *sijills* dealing with the period 1330–1340 (AH) and, for comparative purposes, the *mukhallafat* documents of a generation earlier (several volumes from the period 1300–1310 (AH) to spot trends and changes). The number of cases from 1330 to 1340 is 591, and the number from 1300–1310 is 529. The cases represent the Sunni Muslim community most accurately, but the religious minority communities commonly used the *shari'a* courts as well.

A register, or *sijill,* of probate inventories produced by the *qassam* court typically begins with an inscription like this one:[4]

In the Name of God the Merciful and Compassionate

This seventeenth volume has been renewed for the purpose of precise registry and documentation of the legal estates processed in the Bab Court in Dimashq al-Sham the Protected, center of the state of Syria, the Glorious in the time of our ruler—leader of noble rulers, possessed of tolerance and favor, 'Abd al-Rahman Nasib Efendi in Damascus, Sham the God Protected, and was begun in the month of Rabi' the Second One thousand three hundred and twenty two in the year of the Hijra.

It then proceeds directly to the cases. A typical bound register contains between one and two hundred case entries. The wording, precisely prescribed by formula, reads as follows:[5]

The estate of the the deceased the inviolable 'Arabiyya Bint al-Hajj 'Ali Ibn Amin al-Dayya (the midwife) who having died . . . on the eighth of this month of and of this year in Shaghur in Shama'in Street in Damascus and consigning her legal inheritance to her husband (lord) al-Hajj Rashid Ibn Amin Ibn 'Abd al-Rahman al-Mirayati and in her two children from him, Jamil and Rasmiyya both under the age of majority and in her father the aforementioned Hajj 'Ali and in her mother the inviolable Khadija Bint 'Abdu Ibn 'Abd al-Rahman al-Dahhan and no others . . .

This part of the document thus provides an excellent source of information about names, titles, ancestry, marriage, and children.

After the listing of executors, guardians, and witnesses come the listing and valuation of the estate, giving a glimpse of the objects of consumption and tools of production of everyday life. There follows a list of the items that comprise the estate, starting with clothing and household effects. The items of the inventory are listed in a matrix across and down the page. The name of the item is inscribed with its worth in piasters, or *qurush,* centered directly beneath it in a small, downward-pointing triangle. Arithmetic calculations are pushed to the side of the page. If the deceased's estate consisted of considerable parts of tools, farm animals, books, or jewels, these might well be listed and summed in a separate section. If the deceased owned a store, workshop, or warehouse, there follows a detailed inventory of its contents. Finally, if the deceased was drawing a salary or held significant amounts of cash, these are listed and enumerated. 'Arabiyya's estate consisted of:

Robe . . . 54 piasters
Cotton cloak . . . 100
Old robe . . . 26
Mattress, quilt, and two pillows . . . 171
Tray, basin, pitcher, and small table . . . 150
Wooden box . . . 151
Twenty-one straw pillows, cotton-back cushions, cotton quilt,
    cushion cover . . . 459
Prayer rug . . . 51
Kerosene lamp and porcelain bowls and plates . . . 170
Rug . . . 105
Mirror . . . 110
Bath equipment . . . 12
Pair of shoes . . . 42
Delayed marriage payment (*mahr*) in the care of the aforementioned
    husband by his acknowledgment . . . 500
Total value . . . 2,101 piasters

In the next section all debts, funeral expenses, and taxes are enumerated and subtracted from the total. 'Arabiyya had no outstanding debts, simply the basic fees and expenses associated with the inheritance process.

Court fee. . . . 51
Broker's fee . . . 31
Tax and paper . . . 6
Total . . . 88 piasters

Then each family member is assigned the portion of the total value of the estate allotted to them by the *'ilm al-fara'id,* or science of inheritance. In some cases, a detailed listing of which family member gets which items is included, but in general it is to be assumed that all items mentioned are sold at auction and the profits apportioned. In 'Arabiyya's case, the following shares were assigned:

Husband . . . 493 (received)
Father . . . 329 (received)
Mother . . . 329 (received by her agent)
Minor son . . . 548 (received by guardian)
Minor daughter . . . 274 (received by guardian)

The inheritance document is a simple, purportedly objective list of information that would have been largely confidential while the deceased was alive. It gives almost no information about how the wealth was acquired and how it was subsequently used. It is a dry accounting, but invaluable. This inventory of family and wealth provides insight into the practices of everyday life and of lifetime projects. Reading through thousands of probate cases gives one a two-dimensional familiarity with their subjects and a similarly flat overview of the society. But as various scholars have pointed out, this document set provides an invaluable database of information about all levels of society, and interpreting it requires patience and nuance. It is the only source of precise information about obscure and ordinary people and the only source that systematically attempts to situate individuals in their familial and material context. Contexts, choices, and degrees or quantities of wealth can be discerned and compared, even if narratives, stories, or histories cannot.

The Secularization of Personal Names

Looking at names, we see indications of a population increasingly adopting secular names against more prevalent religious names.6 This constitutes tangible evidence of the process of secularization generally assumed to be one of the hallmarks of Middle Eastern modernization. In general, there is a trend over the course of the second half of the nineteenth century away from the traditional religious names, which formed a very large percentage of the name pool, and toward more secular innovation in naming.

Compared with their own grandfathers, more men who died between 1880 and 1890 had secular names. Eighty percent of the grandfathers had religious names (Muhammad and its variations, names of famous Islamic figures, "servant of God" names made by combining ʿAbd with one of the traditional names of the deity, and Old Testament names), while 20 percent had secular names like Saʿid and Salih. But 72 percent of the men who died in the 1880s—the grandsons—had religious names, and 28 percent had secular names. In the next generation, the men who died in the 1910s, only 63 percent had religious names and 37 percent had secular names.

Within the category of new names arising at the end of the century seen in the 1910s probates, we see new values of modernity represented in secular names. Adib (well-mannered or literary) rises from 1 percent to 3 percent of the total; Kamal (perfect) rises from a fraction of a percent to 2 percent. New names rising to notice include Tawfiq (success) with 3 percent, Sadiq (trustworthy) with 2 percent, ʿArabi (Arab) with half a percent, Nazif (clean) with 2 percent, and Haqi (righteous) with 1 percent. The old-standby secular names most popular among the grandfather generation and reflecting a simpler, premodern set of values declined noticeably. Saʿid (happy) and its compounds falls from 23 to 13 percent, and Salih (worthy) and its variations make up 5 percent of the secular names, after having comprised 13 percent in the grandfather generation.

The trend away from religious names is even more pronounced among women. Of the women whose estates were divided in the 1880s, 47 percent had religious names (mostly the names of women in the family of the Prophet Muhammad) and 53 percent had secular names. By the 1910s, 73 percent of the women who were recorded in the probate inventories had secular names, and only 27 percent had religious names.

The use of titles before a person's name is only a crude instrument for measuring social status, but nevertheless it makes possible an estimate of the percentage of people in Damascene society whose birth, character, or achievements were recognized, acknowledged, and conventionalized in the form of personal address. Based on the probate court records and how the deceased is referred to, information can be gained about titles that were in use and what percentages of the general sample they applied to. Use of titles overall was falling; among those who had titles, religious titles (Shaykh and Hajj) decreased, while the more secularly oriented titles (Effendi and Sayyid) gained ground.

A shaykh was a learned man or head of a corporate group such as a guild or tribe. Just under 10 percent of the 1880s group of men were called Shaykh, but that figure dropped to fewer than 5 percent in the 1910s. A hajj was someone who had made the pilgrimage to Mecca. Of men who died in the 1880s, one-quarter were referred to in the records as Hajj, whereas fewer than 10 percent were called Hajj among men who died in the 1910s. An effendi was originally a designation for an educated person and indicated secular, literate townspeople usually dressed in European style as opposed to the lower or working classes on the one hand and to men of religion on the other. As Hajj and Shaykh declined, Effendi increased among the population of men, rising from just over 10 percent for the 1880s group to one-quarter of the 1910s group. Sayyid (lord) in the classical Islamic tradition referred to a member of the Prophet Muhammad's descent group, but it was increasingly used in the nineteenth century like "mister." Among the wealthier half of the samples, Sayyid was the title for 15 percent in the 1880s group and more than 25 percent of the 1910s group. Finally, in the 1880s group, one-third of the deceased men had no title at all before their names, but in the 1910s group about half of the men had no title.

For women, two titles were used: Hurma and Khanom.[7] The more common (and arguably not a title but a designation) was Hurma. The word hurma means "inviolable" or "protected" and in other usages is joined with the possessive to mean "the wife of." In the legal documents, it is used simply with the woman's name to indicate that she is an honorable, married woman. Khanom designates an Ottoman noblewoman. The designation Hurma declined from more than 75 percent of the women's names from the 1880s to less than 20 percent by the 1910s. Use of Khanom increased (like Effendi) from about 5 percent in the 1880s group to 15 percent in the 1910s group. But the percentage of women who went without a title increased from one-quarter of the 1880s sample to three-quarters of the 1910s sample. As in the practice of naming, we see the practice of recognizing status change almost imperceptibly based on the acknowledgment of the social environment. It is a change many associate with modernity— away from religious and hierarchical status toward titleless homogeneity and status based on new values of literate citizenship and personal sovereignty.

Suburbanization

The data from the probate documents give a rudimentary idea about the relative population size of the various quarters of the city. The population of the whole city at this time has been estimated to have grown from around 150,000 in the 1880s to 350,000 or more on the eve of World War I.[8] Over the years from 1880 to 1920, people's choices about where to live show a population exiting the old walled city in favor of the former garden land in the northern elevations.

Probate records from the late nineteenth century mention the deceased person's neighborhood and street in the formula "*min sukan thumn* [name of quarter], *thumn min athman al-Sham*" (one of the residents of x quarter [literally "eighth"], one of the quarters of Damascus) The appearance of this geographical reference reflects an administrative interest in locating identities in the city that complements reformist efforts to comprehend and control the city by regularizing its subdivisions. Considerable evidence indicates that neighborhood affiliation had been a central element of personal and even political identity of men in Damascus for a very long time, but its inclusion in religious/legal documents represents recognition of that component of identity as administratively important. The loose application of the term *thumn* ("eighth") to more than eight emerging neighborhoods resembles the European use of "quarter" in attempting to project a simple order on a complex, organic urban area.[9]

Thirty-seven percent of those whose estates were divided in the 1880s were living within or just outside of the old city fortifications. Sixty-three percent were living in the outside quarters. Thus, there is a ratio of nearly two to one between the extramural and the intramural quarters.[10] But in the later sample, only 25 percent of the deceased had lived within the old city and 75 percent lived outside it. The two extramural quarters closest to the old city, 'Amara and Qanawat, also showed decreases in population. The difference is neatly made up for in the rise in population—from 17 percent of the total to 35 percent, more than one-third of the sample, in al-Salihiyya, a suburban quarter outside the city walls. It is a startling doubling of al-Salihiyya's representation in the city's population in the space of forty years.

These numbers indicate that in the years between 1880 and World War I, Damascenes were moving out of the old walled city and into the once-independent town of al-Salihiyya and the gardens and agricultural lands between al-Salihiyya and Damascus. This trend was to continue throughout the rest of the twentieth century. There are several possible explanations for this movement. The old quarters were becoming overcrowded and unhealthy. Cholera outbreaks throughout the second half of the nineteenth century and a severe epidemic in 1902 accelerated a flight to the heights of al-Salihiyya on Jabal Qasyun, the mountain overlooking the city. Road construction, increased security through the gendarmerie, and the effects of the new land regimes all helped to open the northern suburbs to families from the inner city.

The movement of residents of the new middle classes and elites of the city toward al-Salihiyya meant a surge in the building of new residences in the garden lands outside the city.[11] New houses increasingly incorporated the distinctive Ottoman style of the late nineteenth century. Instead of the inward-facing courtyard house that shared walls with its neighbors and presented a modest exterior—a style that characterized the inner cities— new freestanding villas outside the new town center of Marja and up the road to al-Salihiyya present the Anatolian *konak* style with a gently sloping roof over a two-story façade punctuated with rectangular glass windows. The inner *qaʿa* or great room, consisting of raised cushioned sitting areas around an entryway with a fountain, was replaced with a *salya* or salon furnished in European style. The plaster geometrical reliefs and painted wood carvings of the grand *qaʿa* were replaced by Ottomanized interpretations of European rococo stylings and wall paintings. These new houses lent themselves less to multifamily sharing, propelling newly married brothers and sons more likely into newly built houses in the same corridor of garden lands.[12]

The Changing Relationship of the Individual to the Ottoman State

Changes in the format of probate inventories in the late nineteenth century signal basic changes in the social construction of the individual. They are related to the Tanzimat reforms of the Ottoman Empire and show the halting effects of sweeping government reform on cultural categories of personhood.[13] The ordinary inheritance document presents an individual in the context of his family and his assets and liabilities. It is the best historical document available for glimpsing the lived reality of ordinary Syrians. In the opening section of the document, a paragraph like block of text, the individual's name, ancestry, honorifics, place of residence and surviving relations are presented. In the next sections, the deceased's possessions are not listed in columns but arrayed across the page in small, neatly spaced, downward-pointing triangles. The name of the item forms the top, long edge of the triangle, and its value in piasters, centered beneath its name, forms the point of the triangle.

In the first decade of the twentieth century, however, the same familiar graphic formula is used for a very different purpose. The introductory block of text informs the reader that this is the record of the belongings of the dead members of the Imperial Ottoman Army who died in a particular *khistakhaneh* (hospital) between particular dates. Then comes the familiar graphic—small triangles arrayed across the page. But instead of the top of each triangle being the name of an item of clothing or furniture, it is the name of a man, an individual soldier. The tip of each little triangle is the usually paltry sum of the value of the possessions on his person at his death. In modern warfare, the dead soldier is represented like an object in the older format. There is no information about his family, place of origin, even his regiment, or the circumstances of his injury and death, only that he, like the companions grouped together with him, died in a particular hospital at a particular time. His legacy is totaled with theirs.[14]

Two hundred and thirty individuals with 7,830 piasters of goods.

Thirty-seven individuals with 185 piasters worth of goods.

Forty individuals with a total of 4,524 piasters of goods.

Fifty-eight individuals with 1,511 piasters worth of goods.

Forty-one individuals with 1,675 piasters worth of goods.

Ninety-six individuals with 3,552 piasters worth of goods.

Two hundred and forty-three individuals with 9,069 piasters worth of goods.

One hundred and one individuals with 187 piasters worth of goods.

One hundred and ninety-five individuals with 841 piasters worth of goods.

One hundred fifty-nine individuals with 336 piasters worth of goods.

Eighty-seven individuals with 1,266 piasters worth of goods.

In a mere eleven records from the years between 1910 and 1920, 1,186 men's deaths and estates are dealt with. This is the most dramatic change to be seen in the content of the second sample of registers. The most dramatic mark of the new century is the graphic representation of men as goods of the state.

Mining veins of comparable information incidentally preserved in inheritance records shows a city gradually changing as people made countless unrecorded decisions about what to name their children, how to address their fellow citizens and where to live and as the nineteenth-century Ottoman state encroached on the traditional public realm of the Islamic courts. The enterprise of datamining, however, which is the window of the contemporary researcher into the past, does not reveal the structures within which the changes were taking place—family, markets, mosques, and governmental institutions. Exploring each of these environments and the values that circulated within them reveals more precisely the dynamics by which the rearrangement and revaluation of cultural capital in structured arenas contributed to the transformations of the end of the nineteenth century. I will undertake this exploration of the trends among ordinary people in their private affairs in the following chapters.

4

BAB AL-MAL:
ON MERCHANT CAPITAL

The exercise of concentrated political capital in provincial reformation outlined in chapter 2 changed the public landscape of Damascus. The equally important changes to private practices—those practices related to property holding and family choices—were decentralized, smaller scale, and made by ordinary people. These changes are visible through surveying the archives described in chapter 3. They were triggered by the increase of trade between Damascus and the Mediterranean coast. An upswing in coastal trade, however, was not in and of itself a direct cause of structural change to the city and its society. Nor was it some magical effect of "western capital" that effected transformation. Rather, the greater availability of liquidity and import and export opportunities to the west gradually changed the investment behavior of many small players in the economy. During the time period in question, trade with Arabia through the pilgrimage (hajj) caravan became less attractive than coastal trade. This reorientation of the primary trade axis from the south to the west had implications for the economy and culture of Damascus.

The experience in the 1850s of Prussian Consul Johann Gottfried Wetzstein, a European investor in Damascus, illustrates the terrain of the Damascene agricultural system and the obstacles to a direct transformation through the infusion of Western capital.[1] Consul Wetzstein was a noted orientalist and the local eyes and ears of the Prussian court in Damascus in 1855. He knew the region well, and, with a state-guaranteed salary that was the envy of local elites in its regularity, was able to purchase rights to two defunct villages in the region of Damascus's Ghuta oasis. They were intended to fund his retirement. But the penetration of European capital into the

Eastern Mediterranean was much more complex than simply buying and improving the traditional landscape.

For 400,000 piasters, Wetzstein purchased the exploitation rights to the two villages. They were—like most of the grain-growing land around Damascus—technically *mal al-miri* (state land), but they were available for exploitation by anyone who was able to undertake the investment and pay the requisite fees. Over the course of four years, he came to regret his entanglement in the complex economy of obligations and dependency.

Along with twenty or thirty other villages, Sekka and Ghassula had been abandoned by their peasantry as economically untenable years earlier. For the peasants, paying *khuwwa* (literally, "brotherhood") or protection money to the Bedouin and Druze tribes from the region of Busra and being victimized by the exploitative practices of Damascus moneylenders and grain speculators had made agricultural labor pointless.

Wetzstein enticed dozens of peasant families back to the land with newly built housing and interest-free loans of seed in the first year, and he allowed them to keep two-thirds of the crop in Sekka and three-quarters in Ghassula. He would pay taxes on the land and fees for the privilege of working the land claimed by the Ottoman state. He bought livestock (forty pairs of oxen and two hundred head of cows, horses, sheep, and goats). In addition to biannual seed money, he lent the peasants money for farm implements and additional livestock at interest rates ranging between 18 and 24 percent. Wheat, melons, apricots, cotton, corn, and lentils were the main crops. Immediately, too, Wetzstein planted one hundred thousand mulberry seedlings to begin a silk-production enterprise in Sekka, and twenty-five thousand grapevines at Ghassula.

Over the next four years, Wetzstein loaned the peasants 60,000 piasters, which they were unable to repay. Marauding Bedouins destroyed large portions of his mulberry and grape seedlings for firewood. Wetzstein eventually banded together with his tenants to pay off the tribes. Ottoman officials helped themselves and the army to food. The mulberry seedlings failed to produce enough leaves for silk caterpillars. Wetzstein was forced to borrow 324,000 piasters, far more than his share of the harvests was worth, from an urban moneylender.

By 1857, Wetzstein was looking to divest himself of his two villages, and he hoped vainly that the local notable 'Abd al-Qadir al-Jaza'iri, the erstwhile leader of the failed Algerian revolt who had settled in Damascus with a huge French pension, would buy him out. Wetzstein used the villages as collateral for another loan of 110,000 piasters to meet his mounting expenses, and eventually he found a buyer who offered him 88,000 piasters for his initial

400,000-piaster investment. This unfortunate example shows that it was not the simple introduction of capital from the West that would transform the Damascene region. On the contrary, the structures and customs of the local economy contained numerous traps for Wetzstein's investment, which drained away any hope of profits.[2]

The reshaping of Damascus and its culture seen in patterns of naming and residence (discussed in chapter 3) began with increased financial liquidity flowing into an established system of value circulation—not that of agriculture, but of trade. The introduction of new levels of liquid money into Damascus had effects on the existing environment—it seems to be associated with declines in interpersonal debt (i.e., trust) and stratification of large and small merchants. Ultimately, it seems to have flowed into the marriage market as well as new real estate building in the gardens outside Damascus and agricultural land outside the city.

How, then, did the Damascene economy change in the second half of the nineteenth century? Incorporation into the Europe-centered world economy was not in any way a direct penetration and domination of the system by European financial capital, in spite of the increasing European investment in infrastructure, which we will examine later. Rather, the transformation was a result of an initial reorientation of the system from the overland Islamic trade region (defined by the pilgrimage) to the waterways of the coastal Mediterranean and the subsequent expansion of the economy with goods and money, which allowed for the realignment of existing patterns of wealth holding.

The Economics of the Hajj Pilgrimage

In 1870, a Damascene Christian, Nu'man Qasatli, lamented the decline of the hajj pilgrimage caravan to Damascus. About eight thousand pilgrims and the 40,000 lira (100 qurush = 1 lira) they introduced annually into the economy were described as abundant streams of gold pouring into the city (*jadawil al-dhahab al-ghazira al-lati kanu yaskubunaha biha dhihaban wa iyaban*).[3] Writing in 1870, Qasatli laments the end of this mainstay of the Damascene economy due to the growth of steamboat travel for Egyptian and other African pilgrims and the opening of the Suez Canal.[4] Travelers who had once stayed and traded in Damascus for weeks or even months now bypassed it altogether.[5]

Isabel Burton's description of the hajj departure from Damascus in 1870 reflects the importance of this ritual movement through the city, and the wealth—financial and other—that the city derived from being a key transit point in the overland economy. Her description, rich in observations of the transitory processional nature of the city's grandest spectacle, also highlights its market aspects. The celebration started with *yawm al-markab*, or the procession of waxen tapers and oil produced in Damascus for the mosques of Mecca and Medina.

> The former articles were carried, not from the mosque, as strangers suppose, but from the place of manufacture in Zukak al-Muballat, which during the last three years has been that of Darwaysh Agha Tarazi Bashi (the head tailor).

The oil, too, was marched from the village southwest of Damascus, Kafr Susa, where it was produced, and Burton notes the prices of the commodity offerings, which were escorted by the best in military and religious spectacles, namely,

> a military band of regulars (Nizam), we counted ten brass, nine flutes, two drums, cymbals and others, . . . a troop of Muezzins, prayer callers of the great Amawi Mosque, led by a Shaykh in a brown cloak with a black hood, . . . [and] seven men bearing incense burners.[6]

The next day, the *sanjak*, or standard of the Prophet was similarly paraded, particularly through the leather goods market in the center of town. The last day of the hajj celebration culminated with the *yawm al-mahmal*, in which an empty litter symbolizing the pilgrimage of the Prophet's wife 'Ai'sha was paraded through the center of town to the southern extension of the city known as the Midan. On this public holiday, the town was full of pilgrims from all over the world, and the local women and children came out to the Midan to see the caravan off. Many locals would accompany it several kilometers down the road to Muzayrib, where a temporary market was held.[7]

The previous description of the three-day event underscores the importance of the circulation of commodities and religious and historical cultural capital into, out of, and through Damascus. It is a celebration of exchange and circulation: Damascus as a transit point, Damascus as a production point, Damascus as a way station in the geography of Islam, Damascus as a market.

The Midan area in the southeast of Damascus grew out along the *qibla* (the orientation of Islamic prayer) toward Mecca and Medina as if specifically for the festive departure of the hajj. It stretches out along former Mamluk parade grounds (hence the name Midan from *maydan*, or the old

Mamluk hippodrome, where horse races and polo matches were held) toward the ritual center of the Islamic world at Medina and Mecca. In fact, the quarter's main function was dictated not by Islamic ritual but by economics. The Midan quarter connected the city of Damascus with the grain-producing regions in the immediate southern hinterland. With grain storage facilities *(baykat)* all along its main route, it functioned as the city's granary. By the late nineteenth century, it had its own court system separate from the others of the city. It was a rapidly growing region, the part of the city where newcomers from the southern rural areas—like the peasants who left Wetzstein's villages of Sekka and Ghassula—would settle. Its aristocracy were *aghawat* (military leaders) who provided security for the hajj and the grain transports into the city against the tribes who made their living by raiding these rich caravans.[8] The Midan was known as one of the city's most volatile and conservative quarters, and its notability may have formed a rival block to the luxury merchants of the inner walled city. This long suburban granary linking the old city to the countryside was the heart of the traditional economy and the conservative mores that went with it.

The Mediterranean Market and Its Pull

Between 1860 and 1913, the tonnage of shipping entering Beirut more than quadrupled, from 400,000 tons to 1.7 million tons per year.[9] By the turn of the twentieth century, Beirut was already well integrated into the Mediterranean market, whereas crossing the mountainous barrier between the littoral and the interior still presented a steep price gradient and profit opportunity for commercial importers. The fact that investors in the new port of Beirut received a 5 percent average annual return on their investment, while investors in the Beirut-Damascus road received a 12 percent average yearly profit, suggests that the movement of goods from the coast to Damascus was the more lucrative branch of the importation route.[10] As Zouhair Ghazzal has argued, capitalist "penetration" did not in itself radically alter social relations in Damascus, but it does seem to have changed the ratio of goods to money and opened up opportunities for a new intermediate class to import goods from the coast and benefit from an inflation in domestic token money, the piaster *(qursh)*.[11]

In addition to the disruption of the hajj trade through Damascus by the effects of new pilgrimage routes on Damascene luxury trade and new mercantile investment opportunities on the coast, the grain trade—which formed the base of the Damascene regional economy (and also was centered in the Midan area)—was also rerouted by the European conflicts in the Mediterranean. At the end of the eighteenth century, the notables of the

Midan had enjoyed a special relationship with the coastal city of Acre and its strongman, Ahmad al-Jazzar, because his port city paid a price for grain well above what it would bring in the markets of Damascus due to the upheavals of the Napoleonic wars.[12] At this point, the notables of the Midan realized that their economic interests might be better served by diverting grain, now a cash crop, away from the city of Damascus through camel caravans to the southern coastal city for transport by sea to Egypt. This set them at odds with the notables of the inner city whose wealth, stored in great *khans* or warehouses in the well-protected heart of the city, were carried overland from the northern and eastern parts of the Ottoman world. This pull of grain to the coast foreshadowed the trends of the late nineteenth century.

While the 1840 Egyptian invasion of Syria by Muhammad 'Ali's son Ibrahim Pasha moved up on Damascus from Gaza, Acre, and Jaffa, there was no road between the coast and Damascus. Traffic was dependent on beasts of burden and good relations with the Bedouin tribes. When the Egyptian gambit for Syria was defeated in 1841 and the hold of Istanbul over Syria reconfirmed, the consolidation of a road between Syria and the Palestine coast closest to Egypt was not an attractive option, because it might facilitate the invader's return. But starting in the 1850s with the Crimean War, there was again much regional demand outside the immediate system for Syrian grain. The Palestine-to-Egypt route was associated with the military pull of Egypt and Britain. The French trade links with Marseille moved north to Beirut with the development of the silk trade and silk production in the Lebanese regions, and for the next decades commercialized wheat export would piggyback on a Damascus-to-Beirut route.

In 1863, the opening of the Beirut-Damascus carriage road dramatically accelerated Damascus's repositioning in the world economy. The French representative of the steamship line Messageries Maritimes, Edmond de Perthuis, was granted a concession by the Ottoman government to build a carriage road from Beirut to Damascus and formed a French company under Ottoman jurisdiction, the Compagnie Impériale Ottoman de la Route de Beyrouth à Damas, to undertake the project. After initial setbacks, the road came into operation, and the arduous three-day journey over the mountains between the coast and the interior was reduced to a mere thirteen hours. This initiated a flow of 11,000 travelers a year, some tourists, but mostly merchants. Between 1863 and 1890, cargo tonnage grew from 4,730 to 21,400 tons per year. The locals called de Perthuis the "amir [prince] of the road." Investors in his company, which held a fifty-year lease and a monopoly on wagon transport on the road, received an average 12 percent profit each year up through the turn of the century, compared with the 5 percent return realized by the investors in the renovation of Beirut's port facilities. Initially, the main export along this road was raw silk, but increasingly the silk entrepreneurs paved the way for grain—the mainstay of the local economy—to become a currency of speculation as much as a foodstuff for consumption in the regional system.[13]

The opening of this road, which predated European investment in railroads by three decades, is key to understanding the reshaping of the Damascene economy. This was not primarily because of the nationality of the entrepreneur and investors, although this was surely indicative of the direction of the pressure. The opening of the road reoriented and rescaled long-distance trade from the Islamic orientation of the pilgrimage, with goods carried overland to Mecca and Medina by thousands of small traders making their way from Eastern Europe, Egypt, Anatolia, and Iran, to the global orientation of accelerating importation of consumer goods from Europe. Furthermore, the road facilitated the export of grain and thus the commercialization of Damascene agriculture. Neither of these trends was initiated by the Beirut-Damascus road; both import of consumer goods and export of grain had begun decades earlier. Trade in both directions, however, was facilitated or accelerated by the opening of the road and wagon traffic.

Production of grain in the dry-farming areas around Damascus increased from 0.5 tons to 1.3 million tons between the 1830s and World War I. The success of the Beirut-Damascus carriage road in the 1860s began linking the two cities not just with consumer goods moving east, but with grain moving west. In the 1860s and 1870s, urban cartels of land controllers actively aided by the Ottoman government directed Hawran grain into the world market. With the depression of grain prices on the world market in the 1870s, it became apparent that the larger regional economy could have devastating effects on the Damascus system. In the 1880s, the grain market fluctuated violently, with grain prices often dismal. Entrepreneurs, rural strongmen, the state, and the peasantry struggled to control the precious food supply. Grain flooded the market, and chronic unrest gripped the rural areas. It was as if the grain and peasantry of the Hawran were being consumed in the process of opening the economy westward.

In the 1890s, the trend was intensified with the French investment in a railroad know as the Damas-Hama et Prolongements (DHP). In fact, the first stretch to be built was from the town of Muzayrib—the site of the traditional hajj pilgrim fair—to Damascus. This stretch was completed in 1894 and extended to Rayak and Beirut in 1895. The DHP railroad formed another link between the wheat production of the Hawran and the larger Mediterranean market.[14] Entrepreneurs could speculate on wheat prices, which had the unfortunate effect of promoting export but also hoarding, and thus destabilizing the local food market and leaving peasants and poor people in difficult circumstances. Because it could fetch better prices on a coastal market determined by outside factors, grain increasingly began to leave the system. Local poor populations were left hungry, angry, and volatile. The Ottoman-built Hijaz Railway, which was completed in 1908 and ran parallel to the French DHP from Der'a to Damascus, had an extension to the southern port city of Haifa. Even as early as 1906, Hawrani grain traders were able to bypass Damascus altogether to set up brokerages in Beirut, and by 1913 Hawrani grain was shipped by railroad to Haifa and then by sea up to Beirut for export, still cheaper than if it had been transported by way of Damascus.[15]

The effect of opening and maintaining new links between Beirut and Damascus was to interrupt the local system whereby the long-distance trade moved through Damascus from Baghdad and Istanbul to Mecca and Medina and grain moved into the city through the Midan corridor. Instead, long-distance consumer goods from Europe were funneled through Beirut to consumption and possession in Damascus, while grain—always the favored medium for speculation of local merchants—was increasingly drawn to the coast for export. This made local grain prices volatile—expensive in the years when there was strong external demand, cheap and unprofitable for its producers when external demand fell short and thus subject to hoarding. The result was chronic unrest among the rural populations of the Hawran and their neighbors at an accelerating pace and increased scale from the 1860s until the turn of the century. The city had always felt threatened by Bedouins; now the threat was from restive peasants.[16]

Grain Out, Cash and Consumer Goods In

The survey of probate inventories allows us to document the expansion of liquidity in the Damascene economy and the development of a commercial-based intermediate class.[17] The new pattern of circulation of commodities imported new consumer goods as well as new cash into the Damascene system in return for grain and, to a lesser extent, silk. There was growth in the amount of merchandise and cash in the system, but the growth was unequally distributed between men and women and among the rich, the intermediate class, and the poor. Different patterns of wealth holding in this most fluid part of the economy differentiated the various strata of society even more as time progressed. Across the board, interpersonal debt relations (and the trust they were built on) declined in a uniform manner due to the greater availability of liquid resources in the market economy. Furthermore, real estate probate transfers became stymied by increasing government regulation. The eventual collapse of the late *tarikat* records as a useful source of information about real estate holdings (around 1911) signals the necessity of looking to other types of sources and texts for information about an increasingly centralized administrative system. Women recede yet further from the historian's view.

An Expanding, Inflating Economy

Comparison of probate inventories of the Damascus archives from the decade of the 1880s with those from the 1910s reveals a dramatic increase in liquid and commercial assets among the population of Damascus. This increase was reflected almost entirely in men's, not women's, estates. It favored the rich but allowed the development of an intermediate commercial class. It may be indicative of growth and/or inflation, and I will refer to the change as a loosening expansion of liquid resources (money and merchandise).[18] A general increase over time of merchandise and money in the estates reflects the increased European trade and traffic with the Syrian coast, especially with the port city of Beirut, and the intensified contact between Beirut and Damascus facilitated by the French-built carriage road between the two cities. It has long been accepted that much of the new liquidity was used by a small percentage of families to acquire rights to agricultural land in the southern Syrian hinterland, thus giving those families control over the critical grain trade in the local and regional markets and enhancing their acquisition of political power.[19] But the new liquidity also influenced the city's cultural structures.

The potential of opening up the Damascus market to the Mediterranean trade is evident in the doubling of the amount of merchandise in the samples of men's estates.[20] The percentage of the samples showing ownership of commercial assets for trade increases from 9 percent of the population before the Damascene market was fully opened to Mediterranean trade to 22 percent afterward. While in the 1880s sample there is a commercial inventory for nearly every twelve individuals in the sample, by the 1910s there is a commercial inventory for nearly every five people in the survey (Figure 4.1). The value of the merchandise in these inventories of commercial assets also indicates an expanding economy, as the piaster value of the commercial assets more than triples (Figure 4.2). The amount of cash listed in the probate estates also doubles (Figure 4.3).

Figure 4.1
Men's Commercial Inventories

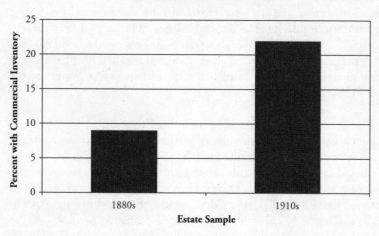

Figure 4.2
Value of Inventories

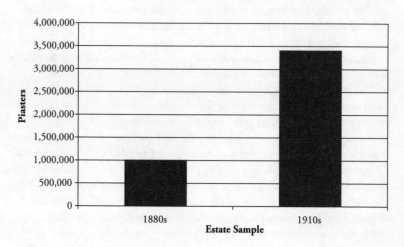

Figure 4.3
Cash in Estates

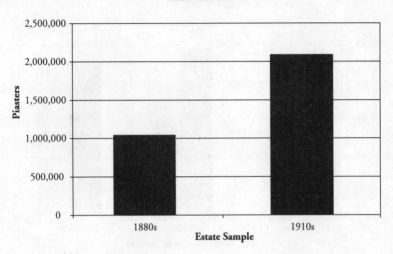

Wealth Strata Trends

This expanding economy, in which cash holdings—analyzed on a theoretical per capita basis—nearly doubled from 1,976 piasters to 3,539 piasters, did not expand equally for everyone in the Damascene population. The way the gains were distributed indicates a new prominence in the liquid expanding economy for people in the middle—a growing new cultural group, a bourgeoisie. Indeed, breaking down the figures reveals different levels of society diverging sharply from one another.[21]

If each sample is divided into a lower part (gross worth below the median), an intermediate part (gross worth below the average), and an upper part (gross worth above the average), the assets of each stratum and gender can be compared for an idea of where resources were being accumulated. When we look at who owned the commercial assets, we see that intermediate men owned the greatest number of commercial inventories—their share of the total increasing from 35 to 44 percent of commercial inventories. Both submedian and superaverage men yielded market share of commercial inventories to intermediate men (Figure 4.4).

Men of all strata were increasingly likely by the 1910s to be involved in commercial activity, as indicated by the presence of commercial inventories

Figure 4.4
Commercial Inventories by Stratum

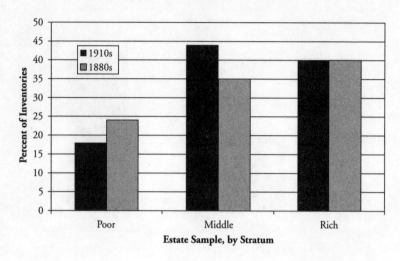

Figure 4.5
Percent of Stratum with Commercial Inventory

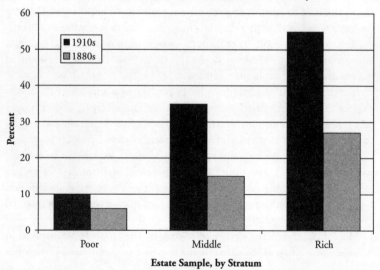

in their estates. The percentage of submedian men with merchandise rose from 6 to nearly 10 percent, while the likelihood of superaverage men being involved in commerce doubled from 27.5 to 55.6 percent of the group. However, the probability that a man of intermediate-range assets would be involved in commerce nearly tripled, from 14.5 to 38.6 percent of the group population. This indicates the formation of an intermediate class based on commerce more pronounced than in the long history of Damascene commerce (Figure 4.5).

The value of commercial merchandise was highly concentrated in the merchandise inventories of the wealthiest men, but the intermediate group gained ground, while the growing submedian stratum lost ground. This indicates that the intermediate class engaged in commerce was beginning to take market share away from the wealthiest as well as the poorest merchants (see Figure 4.6).

Cash was likewise pooling in the coffers of wealthy men, but in this case poor men increased their share of the cash, while intermediate men reduced their percentage of cash by half. This would seem to indicate they had more access to merchandise, while the poor found slippery cash more accessible, and the rich had plenty of opportunity to amass both goods and cash. The new intermediate class seems to have preferred commercial inventories to cash holdings.[22]

Figure 4.6
Commercial Value by Stratum

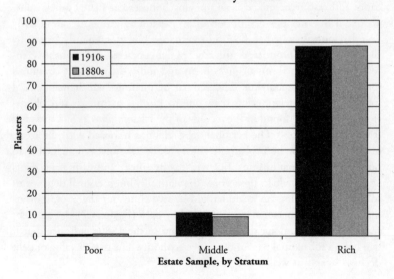

Decrease in Non-Kin Obligations: Debt and Bequeathals

The increased amount of cash and commercial merchandise indicated in the records shows a liquidity of the economy perhaps due to inflation, perhaps due to real growth based on coastal connections and improved provincial infrastructure.[23] The economic changes I see as loosening or increased liquidity are reflected as well in a clear decrease across the board of the traditional economic ties that had bound the economy at an earlier period. The inheritance records show a dramatic contraction in interpersonal debt (*dayn*) and in extrafamilial bequeathals (*wasaya*). These techniques of asset management have the effect of creating nonfamilial social bonds of obligation and responsibility, providing a secondary layer of social structure after the complex web of kinship. Recorded debt and bequeathal declined noticeably for all strata during the period in question. In addition to confirming the expansion and loosening of the economy (no-interest lending is less attractive in times of inflation, less necessary in times of growth), this suggests that property was being closely managed within the family, a trend compatible with the development of the domestic private sphere and the contraction of women's participation in the public economy.

Debt

The double-sided relation of debtor and creditor marks the continuing relation of dependency and obligation between people—quite the opposite of the potential for independent market transactions that commercial inventories and cash represent. It is an ongoing bond rather than a quick transaction. If the previous description of an expanding economy shows fairly liquid resources poised to flow into exchange but momentarily frozen by the death of their proprietors, the array of debt and credit relationships represents more rigid forms of investment and more sluggish and circuitous forms of social transaction. The accrual of interest—which makes debt more a financial relationship than one of human patronage and obligation—is not to be found in the records of the Islamic *shari'a* courts, even if it was taking place.[24] The personal debt relations recorded with the name of the creditor in the probate inventory show relations not reducible to purely financial relationships. But whereas inventory and cash grow, debts and debt levels recede in the records dramatically. Interpersonal debt seems to shrink by half for the wealthier and by two-thirds for the poor, indicating a drop in the personal bonds created by debt (Figure 4.7).[25] That debt was so prevalent among the wealthier strata in the 1880s indicates that it had been a substantial part of the active economy. The piaster value of debt declines steeply as well.

Figure 4.7
Debt by Stratum

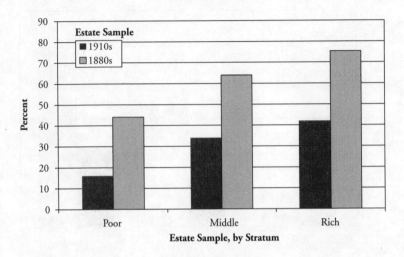

Bequeathals

The Hanafi legal school represented in the probate documents permits an individual to bequeath no more than one-third of the value of his or her estate to a beneficiary or executor (*wasiy*) other than the familial heirs prescribed by inheritance law. Other than founding a *waqf* endowment, this was the only legal technique for preserving the estate's capital from division according to the strict fragmenting rules of Islamic inheritance law, and it requires investment in someone or something outside the family. Like debt, bequeathal *(wasiya)* rates and levels shrink remarkably between the 1880s and the 1910s (see Figure 4.8). Across the board, people were far less likely to make bequeathals and therefore to preserve capital integrity or invest chunks of capital in non-kin enterprises at the expense of their familial heirs. Again, as with debt, the declining trust and extra-kin social bonds made bequeathals seem less attractive investments of the patrimony than letting the assets be divided and flow to family members. Dividing the wealth among a number of family members must have seemed like a better (hedged or diversified) investment in the future than preserving and entrusting up to one-third of it to a project or outside beneficiary in an age of increased liquidity and uncertainty. The decline across the board in debt and bequeathals or non-kin social bonds correlates with a flood of liquidity (part inflationary and part growth) in the public realm and the prefer-

Figure 4.8
Men's Bequeathals

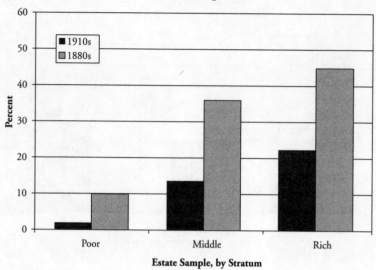

Estate Sample, by Stratum

ence for the privacy of the family as the realm in which value (monetary and social) found a safe haven in times of change.

The decline in non-kin interpersonal bonding also manifests itself in the decline of guilds and the organization of small industrial production. James Reilly's investigation of textile manufacturing indicates an alienation of workers from the rituals and hierarchies of the craft guilds described by Elias Qudsi in his classic work.[26] This phenomenon, primarily seen in textile workers no longer able to compete with European imports, added urban to rural unrest.

Women and Wealth

In both the 1880s and the 1910s, men in general were much richer than women in general. In the 1880s, the average woman's estate was worth 29 percent of the average man's estate. By the 1910s, this had increased slightly, to 32 percent. Moreover, the maximum woman's estate during the first time period was worth only 41 percent of the richest man's estate in the survey. In the second time period, the richest woman was only 38 percent as rich as the richest man. By contrast, the poorest people in both samples were men. This fact is to be taken with a grain of salt; there were certainly many women who had nothing or who had very little (and many with more

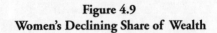

Figure 4.9
Women's Declining Share of Wealth

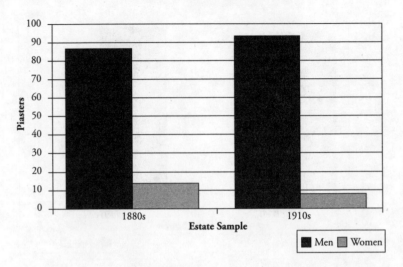

than a little) to their name who simply never appear in the records, but whose estates were divided or absorbed by their families in privacy without accountability to the Islamic law of inheritance.

In fact, the total number of women in the 1880s data set is one-third of the total sample, and for the 1910s the total number of women declines to less than one-quarter. The fact that the percentage of women whose estates were publicly recorded in court declined from a healthy one-third of the sample to less than one-quarter indicates that during the later period, a woman's death and the property transfers associated with it were likely to be handled within the privacy of the family and not in the public arena. Ethnographic evidence suggests that without the strict application of Islamic inheritance law by court officials, female heirs whose rights are usually formally upheld by the courts are the victims of shortchanging and outright exclusion in favor of male heirs.[27]

The sum of the wealth held by men and women in the 1880s sample was 7,198,540 piasters. Women held 13 percent of that (903,258 piasters), and men held 87 percent (6,295,282 piasters). By the 1910s, men's estates comprised 91 percent of the 11,199,141-piaster total in the set, and women held only 9 percent of the total, a sum less than that held by women during the 1880s (Figure 4.9). Only three women's estates in the 1880s and one in the 1910s included commercial inventories. Even if

Figure 4.10
Women's Declining Percentage of Cash

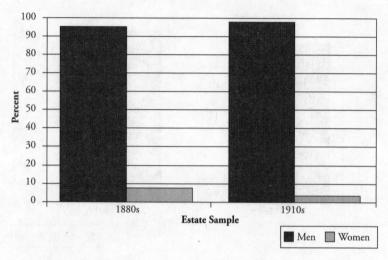

women's property holding was keeping up with men's (which is doubtful),
it was not passing through the probate courts.

A cursory examination of women's cash holdings reveals a sharp difference between men and women and a decline in the amount of cash passing
through women's documented probates. Not only did the total amount of
cash in women's probates decline in absolute terms, its percentage of the
whole decreased by more than half (Figure 4.10). In an interesting contrast
to the men's statistics, by the 1910s the class of women showing an increase
in women's cash was the intermediate stratum (Figure 4.11). For men, this
was the stratum in which average cash holdings decreased as men pursued
other commercial investments.

Real Estate Holdings and Gender

Urban property ownership was the most evenly distributed form of wealth
among the various genders and strata. Overall, 29 percent of the 1880s
sample (both men and women) owned some part of an urban or rural built
structure, a piece of garden, agricultural land, or the rights of use of a building or land (*kedek*). Comparing the real property ownership statistics for the
1880s sample, we find that across strata and gender, a substantial percentage of the people are represented (Figure 4.12). It is interesting to note that

Figure 4.11
Distribution by Stratum of Women's Cash

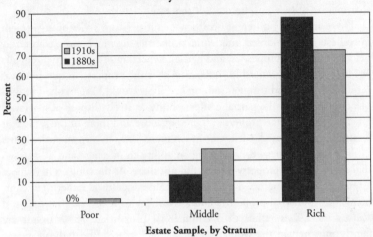

Figure 4.12
Real Estate Ownership by Stratum and Gender, 1880s

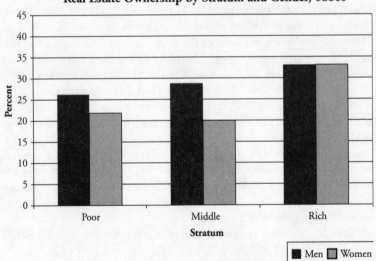

the lowest rate of property ownership occurred not among the poor of either gender, but among intermediate women (the same group of women that increased their cash holdings a generation later).

There are clearly different qualities, quantities, and styles of investment in real estate. For women, residential properties are much more commonly held than income properties, and partial ownership of a property is equally as likely as whole ownership, indicating that the property in question was most likely acquired through inheritance. This would have resulted in serious constraints on the partial owner's ability to freely dispose of her interest. For men, income properties represent more and more of the sample as wealth status increased. Men were much more likely to own an entire house as their wealth increased, indicating an ability to purchase and also to sell that many women property owners did not share. As the subjects have more assets, there is an increased tendency to hold agricultural rather than commercial or industrial properties and a tendency to hold *kedek* licenses and *marsad* mortgages rather than commercial properties. These trends are faintly mirrored in the women's wealth strata as well and indicate that a high level of wealth was correlated with and most likely based largely on local agricultural commerce rather than the new Mediterranean consumer trade that was defining an intermediate class of men.

It is interesting and significant that in the 1910s sample, real estate inventory nearly disappears from the inheritance records, declining to less than 6 percent of all cases sampled from the earlier 29 percent in the 1880s. While it has been challenging for historians to ascertain the effects of Ottoman Tanzimat land reform in the Arab provinces,[28] it is clear that private real property did not simply disappear in the twentieth century, but rather it moved from the jurisdiction of the Islamic probate court to the new provincial government title (*tabu*) office. A *qassam* court register spanning the years 1909 to 1912 shows 25 percent of records listing real estate in the years before 1911 and 0 percent afterward, indicating that the change in the listing and procedural conventions occurred in that year. In another register, from the year 1915, only three cases out of one hundred and forty-six make any reference to real property. Two of the three cases are cross referenced with the new register of *tabu* or title documents, and the third case is the only real-property reference to use new-fangled house numbers to identify the properties in question.[29]

Thus, by 1915, the standards for proof of ownership for inclusion of real property in probate had changed; legal title registered with a new government agency seems to have raised the bar sufficiently for most properties secured with privately held transfer deeds to be at least temporarily held out of probate. In gender terms, this means that one of women's most important sources of wealth, real estate, was blocked from transmission through its most common route, inheritance. If women's ability to dispose of real estate was limited in the 1880s by fragmented ownership, it became one step more difficult with the bypassing of real estate from inheritance court to the title (*tabu*) office. With the passing of real estate transmission from the *sijills* around 1911, we see a further constraint to women's economic freedom and the yielding of the Islamic family, defined by inheritance and the residential patrimony, to the domestic family, defined by marriage and the nuptial chamber.

It was not the direct penetration of Western capital per se that would change the society. The rapid influx of greater liquidity had subtle and complex effects. Consider instead the following account, which shows the adoption of technology by the local elite—the mediation and transformation of imports and their effect on the local landscape. Half a century after Wetzstein's ill-fated venture, the transformation of the system proceeded slowly through the transformation of space by those with a thorough stock of local cultural capital.

We have just set up and started working threshing machine No. 2; it is for Abdul Rahman Basha, the leader of the Mecca caravan (pilgrimage). This machine is something like the one we inaugurated last year on Sursock's farm in the Bekaa, but much nicer, having several improved features. Its straw bruiser has been remodeled; it has automatic feeder, automatic bagger etc. Besides it has a traction engine instead of a portable one. Saturday when the whole outfit had been set up, we hooked the thresher and bruiser to the engine which hauled the whole business through two of the largest thoroughfares in Damascus, and then proceeded to the Basha's property 20 miles outside of the city. It was a really impressive sight to see that rig passing through the city among an exceptionally large crowd, in fact there was present, I was told, as large a gathering of people as on the Mecca procession day. Some people thought that a train had run away from the station and broke into town. The Basha with several friends drove out with us, and seemed very pleased with the demonstration, and with the way the engine moved around. She crushed bridges, but pulled her train beautifully out of the streams. He also, later on, was most agreeably surprised to find the breakage of the grain far below the contract estimate, while the capacity of the outfit in threshing, which was 20 bushels of wheat per hour according to the contract, proved much higher. The Basha and all his friends filled their pockets with samples and then went to Damascus to exhibit them. We wanted to try the bruiser, however we had a small accident; one of the teeth got loose and went to pieces. We have repaired the damage and expect to have everything in readiness by tomorrow. I was very much annoyed at that accident, but the Basha said he was pleased because the machine was almost too wonderful. This little mishap was a protection against the evil eye.[30]

This correspondence from a dragoman to an official of the U.S. Consulate in Damascus in 1903 highlights several aspects of the political economy of Damascus at the turn of the twentieth century. Capital, as it were, is being dragged and driven by a powerful local actor (with the support of foreign power) through the landscape, and the effects were varied and delayed in time. The introduction had to be made in the context of the existing, functioning environment, even as it portended dramatic change for the future. The context for the introduction of the labor-saving piece of equipment is that of cereal agriculture, the traditional mainstay of the economy. The machine itself is remarkable and unusual; it is not part of a wave of mechanization. The people whose labor it will replace flock to see it and mistake it for a runaway train. Its owner is the last of the multifaceted notables to dominate Damascus. 'Abd al-Rahman Yusuf was the scion of a Kurdish military family who held agricultural lands, led the all-important Meccan caravan, and eventually would represent Damascus in the new provincial assembly of the Ottoman Empire. Yusuf and his friends filled their pockets with the new machine-threshed wheat to take back to the markets of Damascus, their main concern as men of means and agricultural proprietors being the grain market. The engine crushed bridges on the road but was able to maneuver through streams with little difficulty. It was set up and regarded quite proprietarily by the functionaries of a foreign power. Its local owner regarded the machine with the destructive power of the evil eye in mind and was pleased that it was not too perfect. The vignette gives a rare moment of insight into the confluence of traditional structures, the Damascene political economy, and the manifestations of global capitalism.

5

BAB AL-USRA:
ON HUMAN CAPITAL

Wealth and children are the adornments of this life.
–Quran 18:46

A man is a blessing, even if he is a just a piece of coal.
—Damascene saying

When a Damascene woman expresses intense and doting love for a son or daughter, niece or nephew, or grandchild, she repeats the expression *enshallah tuqburni* or *enshallah tuqubrini* over and over. Literally, the expression means "God willing, may you bury me." What to outsiders sounds quite macabre expresses love by invoking the most orderly way of death, of the elder before the younger, the mother before the child. It expresses the ideal that the older speaker not outlive the child, that the speaker would not wish to live in a world without that child. It instills in a rough form the child's responsibility toward its elders and those who die before it. It reinforces children's sense of belonging and continuity in the family and in a cycle of life and death. All the emotional intensity of women's intimacy with children is channeled into anticipation of the final moment of contact—God willing, may you bury me. These were not just empty words in a world in which mothers often outlived their children. Family is a "nexus of emotion and interest"[1] and was the immediate context for and pattern of the circulation of the most important cultural capital of all—people.

People's Circulation and the City's Transformation
People, at the risk of stating the obvious, are a society's greatest resource and asset. Like other resources, they move in and out of the city, by birth and

death as much as by migration.[2] People's movements are of a profoundly different character than the exchange of inanimate resources. Irreducible to the mere exchange of objects, they are endowed with purpose, meaning, intent, and sovereignty. Individuals are biologically reproduced at birth, but the fundamental order of family required to nurture and maintain them is reproduced at two other key moments: death and inheritance (with the fission of estates and households, relatives become rival heirs) and marriage (fusion of families). Family is, contrary to its presentation today, a dynamic moving order.

To get an idea of family as a moving dynamic that shapes space, imagine Lefebvre's house—defined as a place by the critical flows of energy (gas, electricity, water) into, out of, and through it. Now think of the house defined by the comings and goings of the people who live in, visit, and violate it. Add births and deaths into and out of it in the days before the institutionalization of these processes, considering that family generally forms the portal by which the system is populated and depopulated. Now take away the house itself—the walls and roof—and watch the of dance of kinship, particular and unique, but iterated over and over, staggered in lifecyclical time, regulated but unpredictable, patterned but unplanned, generative of new people, new families, new patterns of behavior, reproductive of established patterns. Each family node is discrete but woven in with others. To deconstruct this dance, we will look at the two key moments of family reproduction—inheritance and marriage.[3]

Probate Inventories: Family and Wealth

Probate inventories provide some of the only information about family and people as cultural capital, and they illustrate the relationship of family to wealth, which is close but not simple. The family (and the role of the individual within it) was one of the primary sites of the modernization of Damascus; however, it was the most private and removed from the public sphere. In the probate inventories, there is a graphic representation of family as fragmenting and recombining; the family appears as a network, an infinitely variable but structured arabesque of channels through which the accumulated property of a life is distilled and redistributed. The estate distribution documents show a lifetime's concentrated property fragmented and disaggregated over and over; they show the family reproduced and reinforced in shared wealth and the competing but balanced claims of the deceased's patriliny *(ahl al-'asaba)* and his or her dependents *(ahl al-fara'id)*. It is a representation of the moving space of family seen through the highly regular flow of property through it, like a vascular system momentarily revealed post mortem by the injection of dye. We should not mistake the family and material wealth nor imagine that they always imbue each other. On the other hand, Erika Friedl unapologetically assumes that "private property and its social relations, the locus of the production of economic goods, and control of the distribution of surplus goods shapes [kin] arrangements and customs as well as underlying philosophies."[4] Returning to the metaphor of kinship as a dance, imagine that instead of simply removing the walls and ceilings of the houses through which we started our analysis, dancers actually dismantled the house (sometimes in collaboration, sometimes in contestation) and carried pieces (bundles) around with them to rearrange and recombine with others at specific and unpredictable points throughout the dance.

What we will find through the investigation of the court inheritance records is a slow and gradually changing field in which the inflexibility of the Islamic inheritance process as practiced in late Ottoman Damascus does not smother, but indeed enhances the importance of the strategically calculated marriage alliances. Even as people move into and out of the city on other business, the dance of family shaping is composed of two complementary and necessary main motifs—death is an occasion for the breakdown of the family unit, and marriage recombines the pieces into new wholes. Because not just men but also women inherit according to strict rules (there is no variation except to opt out entirely), inheritance is a point in the life cycle where there is little choice or free will to be exercised.

But in such a system, marriage is an opportunity for the exercising of careful and strategic selection. In an Islamic system in which women can and do hold property to different degrees, women are not simply or easily interchangeable as in a society in which they have only fertility and labor to contribute to their households. But Islamic society is not a pure dower society like Jane Austen's England or the Indian caste society, in which the woman's family provides the bulk of the dower to attract desirable husbands. The ambiguous Islamic tradition that the bride's dowry be provided by the groom's side creates a more complex system of recombination. Fission takes place through inheritance, fusion through marriage and the production of the new generation.

Looking at the family as seen through the probate inventories emphasizes that the inflexible regime of inheritance (whose fragmentation of the estate involves enforcing the unpopular and always strained distribution of property to the weak—women and junior men) is complemented by a highly strategic regime of marriage. As Jack Goody put it, "When the bride is a bringer of property or an heir to her father, marriage arrangements take on another hue; it then becomes more important to contract one marriage rather than another, and the profession of matchmaker (primarily a Eurasian phenomenon) immediately becomes relevant."[5] All in all, the picture painted is one of a family regulated by inheritance, innovating through marriage.

This is an important part of the overall process of transformation of the city, at odds with the dramatic narratives and self-consciousnesses of modernists who told and left their stories in which the dimly remembered spaces of childhood confirm but do not explain the process. Family is always the most important vehicle for ordering people—extremely durable compared with the higher-level ordering forms of markets, Sufi *tariqat,* religious *madhahib,* administrative councils, and government projects, which we will encounter in time. Yet the coming together of the Islamic family held in place with inheritance law and the liquidity of the late nineteenth century economy will engender stratification through marriage—in other words, class difference—as we will see in the following section.

Islamic Laws of Inheritance and the Stability of the Family

A cosmopolitan Islamic city like Damascus distinguished itself from the Bedouin tribes and the ordinary peasants in its orbits by the existence of a well-developed legal culture. Islamic *shari'a,* while lacking enforcement mechanisms from the state, was comparatively well developed, a valued hallmark of the high Islamic civilization of Damascus, and in no realm more than that of inheritance. As we will discuss in chapter 6, various forms of religious knowledge including the doctrines of inheritance law of *qisma* were among the primary forms of cultural capital that flowed through and circulated in Damascus, creating the city's identity.[6]

No family was untouched by death and the need to eventually process the estate, and a great many people seem to have availed themselves of the *qassam* (probate) courts.[7] After all, estate division was a complex and sensitive process pitting family members' interests against one another often for the first time, and the legal apparatus living and functioning in the city took precedence over the patriarchal custom and strong-arm tactics that characterized inheritance process where the only authority is that of the patriarchal system.

Because inheritance is very precisely prescribed by Islamic *shari'a,* little can be read into the amounts left by the deceased to various family members. A student of Islamic inheritance procedure, provided he knows what other relatives survived the deceased, knows exactly, without reference to the particular estate, what percentage of her mother's estate a son would receive. The law clearly dictates how the estate should be divided; neither deceased mother nor grieving son has a say if the authority of the *qassam* court is respected. To the extent that some heirs receive variable proportions of the estate, this is due to the presence of competing categories of heirs, not to the will of the deceased. The system is the backbone of the modified patriarchy of Islam, and it is worth elaborating as a model of the channeling of resources.

In the unrestrained patriarchal environment of pre-Islamic Arabia, the deceased's wealth—primarily flocks of livestock—would simply be reabsorbed, poured back into the flock of his tribe, effectively accruing to his brothers, father, paternal uncles, all those who shared his tribal identity and honor, his *'asab.* The word *'asab* means "nerve" and connotes the strict patriarchal system in which men form the permanent skeleton of the descent tree, women leave home to become the vessels of other tribes' reproduction, and women of other tribes are pulled in to reproduce the patriline (except in the cases of cousin marriage, which keeps women within the patriline and consolidates the bonds between brothers). The deceased's women dependents—not members of the tribe but resources of it—far from inheriting, were part of the chattel and would also naturally move to his brothers, father, and uncles as part of the resources in immediate need of protective custody.

The revolution of Islam was to guarantee a part of the estate to a new category of heir, *ahl al-fara'id,* who were not the brothers, sons, and paternal uncles, but those who might previously have been placed at their mercy after the death of the key man in their life—their node in the patriarchal system. The *ahl al-fara'id* are enumerated in the Quran. They are categories of heirs to whom the deceased has an obligation *(fard)*. Interestingly, the word *fard* also means "individual" and in legal contexts refers to an untransferable personal religious duty. As *ahl al-fara'id,* the surviving spouses, daughters, agnatic granddaughters, father, agnatic grandfather, mother, maternal and paternal grandmothers, sisters, consanguine sister, and maternal half-brothers of the deceased are entitled to a fixed percentage of the estate varying from one-half to one-sixth. This category consists mainly of women, the elderly, and maternal relatives most of whom have no juridical relation to the tribe or place in the *'asaba* except based on its patronage.

The remainder of the estate, which may be the major part or may consist of very little after the absolute claims of the *ahl al-fara'id* have been satisfied, is divided proportionally among the male agnatic heirs (the *ahl al-'asaba),* with the nearer agnate excluding the farther. The *'asaba* are the son and his sons, the father and his fathers, descendants of father, descendants of paternal grandfather, descendants of great paternal grandfather, and so on, each excluded by certain conditions. Certain categories of women, such as the daughter and the sister, turn from *fara'id* into *'asaba* heirs if there are male heirs of the same category; in that case, they receive one-half of the share of their male counterparts. Coulson has summed up the complexities of inheritance law into the "golden rule of Islamic inheritance"—namely, that the Quranic or *fara'id* heirs first take their allotted portions, and the male agnate relatives or *'asaba* then succeed to the residue of the estate.[8]

Duty to Dependents *(Ahl al-Fara'id)*

An important consequence of Islamic inheritance law was the regularization of family fission, in spite of the vicissitudes of fate and personality. The effect on the family cycle and wealth of a regular pattern of redivision was a stability and general uniformity of kinship's meaning and value. It is not surprising, then, that the vocabulary of kinship is full of the resonance of obligation and of bonding. The origin of the Arabic word for the nuclear family, *usra,* is that of a bond, an obligation. It is literally related to the word for capture or captivity. The near relations are those who define the limits of freedom and embody the responsibilities that hold one in social place. The common words for father and mother are not those that refer to biological reproduction *(walid* and *walida),* but those that refer to nurturance and fosterage. *Ab* (father) is related to a root having to do with the pasturing of camels. *Um* (mother), which reappears in the concept of *umma* or "community," hints at the ties of emotions and affection that undergird society. It is these words, *ab* and *um,* that are used in tekynymy, the renaming of new fathers and mothers in relation to the name of their oldest son, marking the new parents' passage to full adulthood. Along the same lines, the money paid by agriculturalist villagers to Bedouin tribes for protection is called *khuwwa* or "brotherhood," or in a more specific interpretation the protective, sometimes stifling relationship of a brother to a vulnerable sister or *cadet.* The tie of protection and dependency creates a fiction of kinship between communities.

In contrast to the constricting bonds of the *fara'id, 'asaba* and tribal patriarchy are encoded in the world of general possibility. The word for paternal uncle *('amm)* is closely related to the concept of generality and to the idea of a community. The cohesion of the community larger than the reproductive family is based on a pervasive avuncularity—not the *fraternité* of modernity but a lateral, intergenerational relation of patronage rather than direct succession. The bond is constantly reinforced by the custom of addressing older men as *'ammi* (my uncle) and by men addressing children, reciprocally, with the same term. Husbands and wives address each other as *ibn* and *bint 'ammi,* (my father's brother's son or daughter) even when they are not biological cousins. The father-in-law, too, is addressed respectfully as *'ammi* (my uncle) and the mother-in-law is addressed not as my father's sister but rather as *mart 'ammi,* (my uncle's wife). It is the *patruus* relationship that is primary in orienting the individual outside his or her immediate family. When family means bonds of obligation, patriarchy is the underlying fabric of society.

Limited Strategies of Heirship:
Endowments and Bequeathals

There is a great deal of ethnographic and anecdotal evidence to suggest that Muslim communities and individuals able to do so frequently circumvented the inheritance laws in favor of more customized solutions that favored the strong at the expense of the weak.[9] People wanted to control their legacies through favoritism, but this was very difficult in jurisdictions like Damascus where *shari'a* trumped local tradition except through strategic marriage.

There is practical evidence that people, especially people who controlled significant resources, tended to fight the implication of strict inheritance law through gift giving and endowments. In the records we see that the more a man or woman had, the more likely they were to make a *wasiyya*— a bequeathal or gift—prior to death. In gift giving, particularly that related to real property, a property owner approaching death would "write a house over" to a wife or eldest son so that it would be more likely to remain undivided for another decade or generation. People who owned more property than they needed to maintain their lifestyle had the option of creating a *waqf* or permanent endowment in which the properties or capital became inalienable and dividends were distributed among beneficiaries according to conventions much more flexible than those pertaining to estate division. The foundation of family or pious endowments has sometimes been seen as a device for excluding women. In the end, these strategies merely postpone division, legal conflict, or depreciation of the property and capital.[10]

A person who wanted to control or determine the devolution of his or her accumulated resources could not postpone such action until the deathbed. European primogeniture, ultimogeniture, equal divisions of the estates, and favoritism were not options for the urban Syrian Muslim. Classical Islamic inheritance law severely limits testacy and prohibits it within the family. Reading the probate inventory *sijills* of the *qassam* looking for quirky idiosyncrasies that might reveal changing times is a vain pursuit.

One is impressed with the regularity of reproduction of the complex Islamic family balanced between descent and alliance, *fard* and *'asab*, men and women. As we have seen, the *shari'a* leaves little room for individual choice in the question of capital devolution at death. In only one area of the inheritance process—the bequeathal—can the individual effect a choice that preserves capital integrity from the process of division and family fission.

The Hanafi rite practiced in the inheritance proceedings studied allows one exception to the formal definition of the family through inheritance. An individual is permitted to bequeath no more than one-third of the value of his or her estate to a beneficiary/executor *(wasiy)* who is not one of the heirs prescribed by *shari'a*. The classic Islamic doctrine of *la wasiyya lil warith* (no bequeathal to an heir) prevents bequeathal from becoming a strategy to evade inheritance law or to favor one particular family member. In order to set aside up to one-third of the estate, it must be given to the custody of a nonheir and thus cast outside of the close family. Nevertheless, this is the one direct expression of personal choice in an Islamic inheritance document. The decision to bequeath to a *wasiy* can be interpreted as a preference on the part of the deceased for preserving the integrity of his or her estate (along with strong extrafamilial ties and charitable impulses) at the expense of family members. As we saw in chapter 4, bequeathal declined dramatically as a practice between the end of the nineteenth century and the beginning of the twentieth century, indicating that family division was the preferred route.

Marriage and Family Strategy

Family, in theory, was always a good investment and the most durable of institutions because it was regulated and stable through inheritance law but flexible and improvisational through marriage strategy. The lack of individual control in a court-run probate fission of the patrimonial estate was complemented by the intense selection process and ritual that characterized Damascene marriage. Islam prohibits celibacy on principle and marrying was, according to the long tradition, "half of religion." It is true that people had few options for determining the devolution of their estates, but they did have considerable control over the alliances made through marriage, and with it the ultimate recombination of the fragments of family with suitable fragments of other families. A basic strategic choice was endogamy in the form of cousin marriage or exogamy, marriage outside the patriline for alliance. The highly studied and marked father's brother's daughter marriage of classic endogamy reunited parts of the patrimony separated by inheritance rights of two brothers and rejoined by marriage of their children. Trends toward that form of cousin marriage are deep when the patrimony consists of land or livestock.

The arena of marriage was the setting of more active strategizing as to capital control and devolution. In late Ottoman Damascus, this did not generally mean one's own marriage, but the marriage of one's junior family members. Islamic emphasis on women's property rights and clear compulsion with regard to inheritance can be seen as frustrating to a patriarch's (or matriarch's) desire to pass accumulated capital intact for a single purpose or to a chosen heir, and Damascus is the best example of a community in which the courts and legal system held sway. But because the division and reshuffling of an estate preordain the dissolution of the previous generation's wealth, the parent's strategy becomes how to best recombine the wealth for the strongest potential array of possibilities for the new generation. This selection for recombination—eerily reminiscent of what we now know of the genetic recombination of hereditary capital of genes—is acted out in the rituals of courtship.

Direct courtship—in which individuals engage in the competitive display of their talents, attributes, and material resources before prospective partners to attract a particular mate—is markedly muted in urban Syrian society due to deeply ingrained Islamic traditions of female modesty and privacy. Yet the process of selection is probably more rigorous since courtship is a collective family project that involves calculating material and prestige factors in addition to the potential for mutual physical attraction. An emphasis on the dispassionate and calculating selection of spouses for their children by their families in turn creates a lively market for family reputation and honor. Potential grooms are judged by their capital of wealth, beauty, virtue, and name, which are known by all, while potential brides are sized up by the groom's women folk for their physical assets.

Because a family can engage in a number of strategies concerning the marriage of their offspring, it is all the more important to husband their resources, their marriageable children. They could marry them endogamously (that is, within the male family line with the famous father's brother's daughter paradigm or variations of it) to preserve patrimony and solidarity or marry them exogamously (outside the family) to increase alliances with the outside world. In Damascus, marrying out seems to have been a valued norm, and the process by which families sought outsiders to marry their members shows gender marking of the streets between homes. Two of the most ritualized gendered and purposeful movements of people through the streets are related to marriage and show the patterned linking of households.

First is the scouting of the *khattabat*, or "matchmakers," described here in its late nineteenth century form by Khaled Chatila:

When a young man reaches the age of marriage, his family begins to prepare, careful above all to avoid all breaches of custom and propriety. But because in the cities the women wear veils and there is strict separation of the sexes, the young man cannot himself choose his bride, and this forces him to depend on his relatives in this delicate area. That would normally be his mother, his aunts, his grandmother and his sisters who play the essential role of intermediaries. After having asked the future bridegroom what kind of bride he would prefer—blonde or brunette, big or small, thin or plump—they begin their quest without delay. At first they inform themselves about the marriageable girls who would appeal to their relative. They get this information from their friends and acquaintances. When they feel themselves sufficiently informed, they put on their best clothes, they begin their campaign, knocking on the doors of the indicated houses, without notice and without having announced themselves. They are called *khattabat* or "marieuses." The houses open themselves up wide before them, and everywhere they go they receive the warmest and most courteous reception. Etiquette demands that they not immediately reveal the object of their visit. In the beginning they simply exchange pleasantries with the mistress of the house.[11]

Women of the groom's family direct this ritualized mode of shopping for and selecting a bride. The next phase of negotiations is one in which the senior women negotiate the *mahr* (marriage payment or gift), and the final agreement, having been worked out by the women, is turned over to the senior men of the family for a formal conclusion. The formal visit by the men to settle the contract was the second ritual movement from household to household—a *wajaha* (spectacle or face-off) in which the goal would be to assemble as many high-status male family members and residents of the neighborhood to speak to the father of the bride on behalf of the groom. The more status capital assembled by the groom to be in his *wajaha*, the greater the honor and pressure to the family of the bride. Technically the consent of the bride is mandatory in Islam, but her silence had the legal status of consent, and her father might assent to the marriage with words like *i'tibruha khadma bi matbakhkum* (consider her a servant in your kitchen).

Investing in Family: From Patrimony to Matrimony

The data patterns analyzed in chapter 4 show an economy expanding with commercial merchandise and money and an associated decline of networks of extrafamilial economic bonds. The decline in bequeathals signals that the *qassam* court and fragmentation of the estate among family members were a better bet for the uncertain future than capital integrity. In these changing times of economic expansion and administrative reform, people tended to prefer devolution to family members as defined by Islamic inheritance laws over bequeathal, borrowing, or lending of money outside the family. Fewer people invested in social relationships bound with debt, and fewer diverted money via bequests away from their familial heirs. The sudden disappearance of real estate devolution from the record in 1911 and the gradual shrinking of women's percentage of estates and women's active participation in the economy suggest that the accountability of the patrimonial family to the inheritance courts was also in recession. Analysis of the corresponding data on marriage payments from the two samples of the 1880s and the 1910s reveals rapid change in the formation of the matrimonial family.

Mahr is the payment Islamic law requires that the groom make to the bride. In urban Damascus, the *mahr* is usually divided into two parts, one payable at the beginning of the marriage, the *mahr muqadam,* and the other, the *mahr mu'akhar,* set and pledged to be paid at the termination of the marriage by divorce or death. The probate inventories, occasioned by the death of one of the parties to a marriage, only show information about the *mahr mu'akhar,* or the delayed part of the marriage payment.[12] When the deceased is a man, the *mu'akhar* is recorded as a liability against the estate. When the deceased is a woman, the *mu'akhar* is recorded as a credit to the estate.

Until the late 1980s, most anthropology of marriage transaction systems was primarily concerned with categorizing societies as either bridewealth or dowry types and identifying the essential socioeconomic characteristics of each type. In the far more common bridewealth systems, wealth moves from the groom's to the bride's side, circulating wealth laterally in societies with little private property or stratification. In the far rarer dowry systems, wealth moves from the bride's to the groom's side through the new household and through offspring, concentrating and directing wealth descent over time. The dowry system tends to be associated with societies characterized by private property and class distinction. Put another way, bridewealth circulates wealth laterally in societies where women's labor and fertility are key to subsistence; dowry concentrates wealth in societies where the means of production is less tied to women's contribution to subsistence and rests in other modes of production.[13]

But like European historical studies of the dynamic relationship among inheritance, dowry, and wealth, Islamic *mahr* problematized the system whereby cultures were assigned to one static and essential category—either bridewealth or dowry. It is more helpful to view marriage transactions as strategies, therefore as flexible and evolving. Indirect dowry is the anthropologist's term for Islamic *mahr*, which combines aspects of bridewealth and dowry.[14] Like bridewealth, it is paid by the groom's side; but like dowry, it goes to the new household, and specifically to the bride and her heirs (not as compensation to her father and brothers, as in typical bridewealth systems). As such, indirect dowry has historically been seen to be flexible across cultures, with some Islamic societies emphasizing the bridewealth aspects, others the dowry aspect.

The adaptability of Islamic *mahr* to approach either bridewealth or dowry practices must have facilitated the Islamicization of different types of societies from Africa where bridewealth practices dominated to India where dowry was the norm, and it seems to have facilitated cultural differentiation in stratifiying societies such as late Ottoman Damascus. Both anthropological studies and historical studies provide evidence that in stratified societies, bridewealth and bridewealthlike transactions are prevalent near the bottom of the social pyramid, while dowry and dowrylike transactions emerge in the upper ranks.[15] Judith Tucker's preliminary work on *mahr* and class in Nablus has indicated that it looks more like bridewealth in poorer classes and more like dowry in wealthier classes.[16] The Damascus data show that the dynamic tension between the bridewealth and dowry aspects of *mahr* produced an intermediate class, revaluing women and illustrating different male investment strategies in the uncertain expanding economy.

In contrast with conventional wisdom that sees the Islamic family as static and unchanging, this analysis shows that over the period of a few decades, Islamic marriage practices in Damascus differed considerably by wealth stratum and adapted themselves to accommodate the expanded liquidity described in chapter 4. Over time, the data show that the dowry-based marriage for alliance, traditionally practiced by the upper stratum, began offering men from the submedian wealth stratum an attractive investment for their increased but precarious liquidity. This is notable at a time when economic investment is undermined by the political instability of administrative reform and the unknown horizons of a newly liquid economy. Thus, by the beginning of World War I, ordinary men were directing increasing amounts of money to "marry up" to women from families whose daughters carry a "dowry" of social prestige and connections. An emerging intermediate class absorbs new liquidity brought by ordinary men to secure alliances with women endowed with social capital. The result is a changing gender ideology emphasizing domesticity and patriarchy and a new middle class born of new money and old prestige that will pointedly nurture the "deep horizontal comradeship" of nation.[17]

Mahr Mu'akhar: Stratification and Inflation

The *mahr* credits for women in the 1880s show that the *mu'akhar* for the wealthiest stratum of Damascus was almost three times as much as for women in the intermediate stratum, which in turn was three times as much as for women in the lowest stratum. Even more dramatically, the *mahr* credits for the superaverage women ran up steeply (66 percent) by the 1910s, but those for poor women hardly budged (9 percent) (Figure 5.1). The pattern for superaverage women indexes an increasingly dowrylike *mahr* culture—marrying the right woman at any cost (or rather at nine to fifteen times the cost of an undistinguished woman) is very important in a society in which women inherit, own property, and bring distinction and prestige. The pattern for submedian women indexes a brideprice-like *mahr* culture in which women's labor and fertility are more important than their property and distinction, women are more or less interchangeable, and they have

Figure 5.1
***Mu'akhars* Owed to Women (by Stratum)**

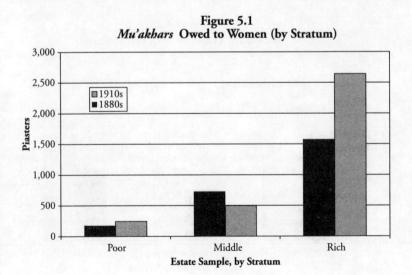

a fairly stable "price" (200–250 piasters). This is a clear indicator of accelerating stratification—the most desirable women are "bid up"; an ample supply of undistinguished women keeps the "price" minimal.

At first blush, one would expect that the patterns of what men owed would mirror the patterns of what women were owed, but this is not the case. Submedian men initially owed twice the average of what submedian women were credited with, and this average rose dramatically (136 percent) over time. Intermediate-stratum men, too, owed more than what intermediate-stratum women were owed, although the difference was not as dramatic as with poor men. Finally, superaverage men, in contrast, did not owe as much on average as superaverage women were owed (Figure 5.2). The men's patterns show that wealthy and intermediate men contributed to the dynamic of stratification by bidding up *mahr* levels for well-endowed women. But wealthy men could afford to and did marry "down" for more moderate *mahrs* without sacrificing their social position, resulting in an average less than that commanded by wealthy women.

The most interesting statistic, however, is the statistic for the poorer half of men. This group pledged twice the average amount that poor women received in the 1880s and ramped up that demand 136 percent by the 1910s. The best way to read this puzzling but striking trend is that it was primarily demand by submedian men who were pushing the *mahr* levels for elite women higher and higher in an attempt to imitate the strategies of the

Figure 5.2
Mu'akhars **Owed by Men (by Stratum)**

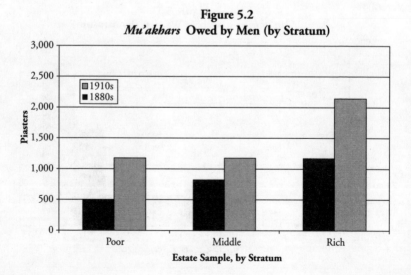

Estate Sample, by Stratum

better off—to ally themselves through marriage with traditionally powerful families and to vault from the stratum of labor, interchangeable women, and lateral circulation of cash to the stratum of property, distinction, and prestige potential in uncertain times. There was a perception that marrying the right woman and thus forming the right social alliance was the most important investment a man (with new money to invest) could make. It was a preferable mode of diversification of commercial gains than lending or bequeathing capital. That the men who invested at a level of 45 percent of their gross probated assets to secure unions ended their lives in the sub-median stratum means that the strategy of marrying up did not generally work as a wealth-enhancing technique. Imitating the wealthy by investing in marriage alliances did not raise the economic standard of submedian men but promoted stratification and distinction. Individual investments did not necessarily create successfully bourgeois households, but collective-ly created new values for women and men and a class of mixed-stratum households with new gender-related tensions.

By the 1920s, the uncontrolled inflation of *mahr* payments was recog-nized by the new bourgeois intellectuals as a serious problem in Damas-cus, and an action committee dedicated to lowering *mahr* levels was formed in 1928.[18] The committee deplored the wastefulness, blind imi-tation of high society, and impracticality that it saw as causing the rise in *mahr* levels, manifested and driven by the intermediate and upper classes to spend huge sums on elegant dresses, multiple pairs of shoes, dozens of undergarments for the bride, and luxurious furnishings for the nuptial chamber or house. This anxiety about fashion, luxury, and materialism complements the rising discourse of domesticity—thriftiness, economy, virtue, and housekeeping—evident in the Egyptian and Syrian local press.[19]

The most striking data show the steepest changes in a group's average *mahr* over time in the *mu'akhar* payments owed to superaverage women (66 percent) and owed by submedian men (136 percent). The average owed to a rich woman rose 66 percent—the competition for the society's best-endowed females was thriving. These most-desirable women brought with them to a marriage not just their bodies, their labor, and their fertility, but also their natal families' wealth, name, connections, and prestige. But the average owed by the poorest men rose more than twice as fast—136 percent between the 1880s and the 1910s. In these statistics, we see a competitive urgency to turn the newly accessible liquidity of the society into something a bit more durable: alliances with daughters of well-placed families. Even the poorest men of the society—or rather, *especially* the poorest men of the society—had an incentive to invest an average of 45 percent (by the 1910s) of their ultimate assets in marriages. The incentive: unpredictable times, changes in the political economy, increased liquidity or inflation of local token currency, deflation of the regional economy, and the decline of personal bonds of debt and credit. The fact that these men ended their lives in the submedian category of wealth—poor and heavily indebted to their wives—indicates that the strategy was not particularly successful. Bourgeois domesticity was not a safe haven, hedge, or guaranty against the unprecedented economic contraction of World War I. But it was ordinary men, flush with the slippery liquidity of the new economy, who most contributed to the new market culture that put some women on a pedestal while debasing the majority of them. The statistics show a growing class of submedian men and an economy sloshing with liquidity and retail commercial inventory chasing a shrinking class of women. This models classic inflation of gender values and real growth and development of a durable middle class.

With men's natal family resources and commercial liquidity being increasingly invested in ambitious marriages for sons, daughters of submedian families formed a pool of women who could be married off for very low, nominal *mahr* payments. These women had little or no family prestige or influence to offer their husbands—just labor, companionship, and fertility—and over time, they represented a financial liability to their parents and siblings as they aged out of the marriage market by their mid-twenties. By the 1910s, it is not surprising that the number of women in the sample who are not survived by any children more than doubles for each stratum of women, and the number of submedian women whose records show no trace of husbands, marriage, or children more than triples by the latter time period. In the 1910s, women without marital families in the tight new marriage market make up a striking percentage of each stratum and of the whole, as women embedded in matrimonial families recede from the public record into bourgeois domesticity, whose legacy from Islam is privacy and invisibility, not patrimonial rights.[20]

Interestingly, by 1920, the average women's *mu'akhar* represents 16 to 17 percent of her assets, regardless of which wealth stratum she belongs to. The pledged *mu'akhar* represents a lower percentage of total assets for poor and intermediate women in an economy full of cheap consumer goods, and a higher percentage for wealthy women as their status outruns the sum of their material wealth. Thus, by the 1910s, knowing a woman's *mu'akhar* would allow an analyst to predict her gross estate value and material consumption patterns. Commodification and homogenization of women's values develops, despite—and, indeed, through—dramatic stratification.

Conclusions:
The Precarious Foundations of National Values

Initially, in trying to make sense of the conflicting trends in men's and women's outstanding *mahr* payments, I was tempted to regard the difference in the lower wealth sectors as indicative of a classic brideprice pattern, in which the difference between what men pay and what women receive is a de facto transfer to the bride's male relatives, a hidden payment for her labor and fertility services, a lateral circulation of value in a fairly homogenous, male-dominated society. This was clearly not happening at the family level, however, as it would have violated both the letter and spirit of the *shari'a*. (We are dealing, after all, with the courts of a highly developed Islamic legal subculture and with the population that chose to use them, not with marginal tribal custom.) And yet at the level of wealth strata (classes), a bridewealth model for these lower sectors is still appropriate, as there is an overall outflow of money from the strata of submedian and intermediate men to those of intermediate and superaverage women.[21]

The top sectors of society, by contrast, show a different pattern. The average *mu'akhar* payments of the society's top women are more than what the society's top men are paying in. In classical anthropology terms, this looks like dowry—a net transfer of value from the bride's side to the groom's side, again at the level of class, not necessarily household. The bride brings a nonmaterial (but very valuable, especially in the liquid expanding economy) dowry of prestige and connections, as well as any property interests she might inherit, from her natal family to her husband's children.[22] The trend to a dowry system can further be seen in early twentieth century adaptations like the trousseau of matching funds *(jihaz)* provided by the bride's family or the renunciation of material *mahr* but for a symbolic single gold coin or a *mushaf* (copy of the Quran). This indicates the simultaneous material self-confidence and social anxiety of families whose daughters were literally "too good" for the market, "priceless," and who would have run the very real risk of not finding a suitable match had they attempted to quantify their family's prestige.[23]

What we see, then, is a marital dynamic different from but fed by the influx of merchandise and liquidity documented previously, which also wove together an intermediate stratum of mixed households. Wealthy brothers, whose sisters commanded the highest material investment in marriage from their suitors, were already at the top of the social pyramid and could confidently marry beneath their wealth and status position without damaging their own social standing. In an edgier combination, poorer men poured resources into securing alliances with high-prestige

women to preserve their liquidity against erosion. In either case, the resulting households created by these strategic, stratifying marital dynamics
would have nurtured national discourses and values that emphasized ide-
alized values of patriarchy, fraternity, domesticity, and men's and women's
places in society as new generations processed, rationalized, and justified
the differences in social origin and style between their mothers, fathers,
aunts, and uncles.

The new middle class which national sentiment of the twentieth century would inhabit was not a common brideprice world of horizontal homogeneity resting on women's labor, nor was it an elite dowry world where
women competed outright for the wealthiest men. Instead, it was a dynamic conjunction of cheap liquidity and precious femininity, where fixed
Islamic patrimony gave way to the bet on domestic matrimony as the perceived safe haven for value. The effects of this development included the
standard "pricing" of several classes of women within the marriage market,
the exclusion of many poor and some rich women from the new family, the
increasingly strict gender segregation of the public and private spheres, and
a thriving of discourses of bourgeois domesticity. This tense new middle
class would lead Ottoman/Islamic Damascus into the national age.

6

BAB AL-'ILM:
ON INTELLECTUAL CAPITAL

Chapters 4 and 5 focused on the changing patterns of circulation in two realms of the private—private property and the privacy of the family. Chapters 6 and 7 will illuminate patterns, dynamics, and trends in the public sphere—not where capital is secreted and accumulated, but where it is spent and exchanged. We will start the investigation again in the archives of the probate court to get some tangible data as a starting point on intellectual capital in the form of libraries. Eventually, however, we will move away from the lists of book titles to the possible application of the books in the world of politics. In contrast again to chapters 4 and 5, when examining the intellectual capital visible in the probate inventories we find that it is remarkably stable, unchanging, inelastic, and illiquid. In comparing the inventoried libraries of the decade of the 1880s with the decade of the 1910s, we see neither an expansion in the number or type of books nor an expansion in the sociology of book owners. This observation was particularly surprising, since I had expected the clearest signs of modernity in the probate inventories to be an expanding number of readers, titles, and genres. Instead what I found was a literary tradition of Sufism with limited scope which nevertheless served as a stable interpretive lens for a small community of thinkers over a half century of change. The durability of the Sufi literature as a value seems be linked to two important developments: (1) the change in identity of its readers from Sufis to reforming proto-national Salafis and (2) the floating of an alternate form of Sufi identity based on *taqlid* (tradition or imitation) rather than the *ijtihadi* (reformist) strain of the Salafis.

Book Ownership at the End of the Nineteenth Century

Out of more than two thousand *mukhallafat* documented from between 1880 and 1920, only thirty-three,[1] or about one-tenth of 1 percent, contained book collections. Even if allowance is made for collections kept in family common in a mosque or *madrasa,* it is clear that book ownership was not a mass phenomenon. None of the book owners were women, although women formed nearly one-third of the entire sample. A rough class analysis revealed a nice bell curve. Nine percent of book owners were otherwise destitute, including a soldier who died in the Hawran campaigns of the 1890s and an heirless shaykh who made a living practicing various occult arts. Likewise, 9 percent were very rich, including the last really powerful Hanafi Mufti of Damascus, Muhammad Hamzawi, who died in 1886. Eighteen percent of owners were lower middle class, 21 percent were very well off, and 42 percent fell into the range of wealth that I identified as the middle class.[2] This suggests that book collection was part of an upwardly mobile lifestyle and not simply a manifestation of wealth. More than 80 percent of the value of books owned was in the hands of the lower middle, middle, and upper middle classes, and the lower and middle classes held 38 percent of the total value of books, almost as much of that value as the upper middle class, which held 42 percent.

In the overall sample, more than 90 percent of the books were in Arabic. Ottoman Turkish was a distant second language, with no more than 8 percent of the sample. The third-favorite language was French, which appeared mostly in the form of language instruction books. Farsi and Russian barely registered. It must be emphasized here that these are Muslim people's collections, and the inclusion of libraries of minorities would probably present a very different picture. Incidentally, there were only two identifiable Arabic translations of European works among the stock of the one bookstore owner in the sample. These were translations of the French tragedy *Télémache* and of Dumas' *The Count of Monte Cristo.*

In the total sample, there was very little overlap with the lists of books known to have been printed by the six or seven presses of Damascus in the nineteenth century.[3] The only significant overlap was with the output of the Syrian Provincial State Press. Several collections contained a copy of the Constitution, the *Majalla* or civil code, The Land Law of 1858, The Commercial Laws, and the Health Code. It is worth asking where the other products of the Damascus presses were being sold—perhaps they were cheap and low prestige and thus relegated to the piles of unnamed books sold in bulk from all the large collections. Most of the literary and scientific works came from Beirut or Istanbul, while the religious works were either in manuscript form or had been printed in Cairo, some by the famous Miri Imperial Press. Manuscripts formed much of the collection of the highly positioned *'ulama*. In one of the richest collections, whose owner died in 1885, two-thirds of the value of the collection was in manuscript form. Among laymen, only two people who died in the earliest years of the survey owned a few costly manuscripts. As non-*'ulama* acquired more texts, they acquired them in the form of printed books.

Professionally, the book owners broke down into three classes. *'Ulama* made up 55 percent of the sample, military officers made up 12 percent, and merchants made up 33 percent. One hundred percent of the military officers owned books in Ottoman Turkish—from the Arab captain killed in action whose only book was a Turkish grammar to the pasha and agha who were connoisseurs of modern Turkish poetry. Language learning was obviously important to this group of readers. The battalion commander, who was an avid collector of books in Turkish, seems to have been teaching himself French.

Civilian laymen responded steadily to the availability of affordable printed works from Beirut and Cairo. These collectors from the early part of the sample looked in their collection patterns like minor *'ulama* with expensive, multivolume sets of religious books. Toward the end of the sample time period, they have their own distinctive patterns of diverse single-volume acquisitions.

Unsurprisingly, the survey is dominated by the *'ulama*.[4] Religious scholars owned nearly 60 percent of the total value of books in the period, with two-thirds of that figure being held by prominent *'ulama*—muftis, holders of endowed teaching positions, and a Sufi shaykh. The bulk of an *'alim's* library was made up of commentaries referred to in the records as *hawashi*. These are comments upon comments upon comments of a *matn* or original text. The fact of the predominance of this form of religious literature is significant. It is the collection of *hawashi* commentaries that marks the traditional religious scholar and sets him off from the ordinary effendi as a reader and book owner.

The number-one best seller of the time period was, as expected, the Quran—referred to in the documents as the *mukaram al-sharif* (the noble holy book). It was present in one-third of the collections. This figure may at first glance seem surprisingly low, considering the centrality of religion in the profiles of the book owners and the bulk of their reading materials, until it is recalled that this literate subsection of the society would have been likely to know the Quran, or parts of it, by heart, and that a substantial percentage of those who did not own a Quran owned a set of *tafsir* that contained the holy text within it. The Quran was, after all, primarily an oral and aural experience.[5]

The failure to own a Quran is most noticeable among the *'ulama* class. Ottoman military officers and non-Damascene *'ulama,* on the other hand, tended to own multiple copies (one officer seems to have owned eighty-eight Qurans), and they tended to treat them in a more talismanic way—for example, using the expression *wahbet al-mushaf* (gift of the holy book) in their inventory accounts to avoid the notion that the word of God was being bought, sold, or valued in monetary terms. This expression was never seen in the documents pertaining to native-born Syrians.

Somewhat surprisingly, the Quran was tied for first place by *Maqamat al-Hariri*—a medieval work of moralistic animal stories known for its linguistic and poetic virtuosity. The fact that this work, whose author feared it would be regarded as frivolous, was as widely spread as copies of the Quran in this community indicates a deep appreciation for the Arabic language and literary heritage in the generations before Arab nationalism.[6]

The presence of Sufi literature in nearly three-quarters of the sample was the most striking trend of the survey (see Table 6.1). The only Damascene authors whose names came up repeatedly were its great mystics: Muhy al-Din Ibn 'Arabi, 'Abd al-Ghani al-Nabulsi, Shaykh Khalid Naqshbandi, and 'Abd al-Qader al-Jaza'iri (see Table 6.2).

But the works of 'Abd al-Wahhab al-Sha'rani outstripped even these Damascene classics. The fact that several of al-Sha'rani's books were printed in Egypt in the middle to late nineteenth century in several different editions certainly contributes to this statistic, but so does the fact that his work addressed general questions that would have been at issue in times of transformation for the Sunni community. Al-Sha'rani is covered in a few pages in introductions to Arabic literature[7] and to Sufism and is remembered in this literature as a conceited and mediocre—but prolific, somewhat original, and honest—writer.

Table 6.1
Book Collections with Sufi Works

Description	Number of Collections	Percentage
With Sufi literature	24	73%
Without Sufi literature	9	27%

Table 6.2
Sufi Writers Present in Book Collections

Writer	Number	Percentage
'Abd al-Wahhab al-Sha'rani	15	45%
'Abd al-Ghani al-Nabulsi	12	36%
Shaykh Khalid	4	12%
al-Suyuti	10	30%
al-Ghazali	8	24%
al-Qushayri	7	21%
Ibn al-'Arabi	9	27%
'Abd al-Qader al-Jaza'iri	2	6%

'Abd al-Wahhab al-Sha'rani's life spanned the end of the Mamluk period and the onset of Ottoman rule in Egypt. It is not inappropriate that one of the best sources and commentators on the early days of Ottoman rule in Egypt would be the most popular author in the last generation of Ottoman rule in Syria. His works contain advice on the pragmatics of the relations between shaykhs and princes, a spirited attempt to unify the four main schools *(madhahib)* of jurisprudence, harsh critiques of fake and ignorant Sufi shaykhs and of corruption within the popular Sufi orders and of the dry legalistic 'ulama (whom he likened to donkeys carrying books they cannot comprehend),[8] praise and respect for his own illiterate Sufi master, and many other ingredients of what would contribute to, in the next generation, Damascene Salafism or Islamic reformism.

Al-Sha'rani has been studied as an example of medieval Sufism, and his works have been cautiously read as historical sources on early Ottoman Egypt.[9] But it is worthwhile to try to piece together a picture of how and why al-Sha'rani was being read in another society undergoing traumatic change and attempting to reconfigure itself nearly four hundred years after al-Sha'rani lived.

As al-Sha'rani's works were published in Egypt by the Miri Press and quickly circulated in Damascus,[10] parallels between his time and late Ottoman Damascus were developing. Al-Sha'rani's life spanned the end of Mamluk and the onset of Ottoman rule, and the end of the nineteenth century saw the modernization and Europeanization efforts of the Tanzimat. While early sixteenth century Egypt grappled with the changes wrought on world trade and Egypt's role in it by the opening of new trade routes, late nineteenth century Syria underwent the symptoms of its entanglement in a new global industrial economy—the flood of European imports, the unprecedented opportunities for grain export in the 1850s, and the world recession of the 1870s. In al-Sha'rani's time, tension exploded in the mistreatment and massacre of *dhimmi* minorities, and the Lebanese and Damascus massacres of Christians in 1860 brought up questions of responsibility and morality within the Syrian Muslim community. In both cases, ordinary people would have looked to traditional religious authorities to lead them through and to help them understand the shifting modalities of power. Both periods of change brought into question the importance of traditional *ulama* and their relationship to the state. But this does not tell specifically how or why al-Sha'rani's work came to be read and contested.

The Naqshbandi Sufi Order and the Salafis

The owner of the largest collection of al-Sha'rani's writings and of Sufi literature in general was Muhammad al-Khani the younger, the head of the Naqshbandi-Khalidi order from the 1860s until his death in 1898.[11] His biographies highlight the fact that he studied and was certified in al-Sha'rani's works, including ones that do not appear to have been published at the time.[12] In addition to being the main purveyor of Sufi literature and al-Sha'rani's works in Damascus, Khani was at the center of the small group of older *ulama* whose authority remained intact in the aftermath of the massacres of 1860. He was the mentor of the subsequent generation of scholars who ultimately rejected Sufism, as well as traditional jurisprudence, in favor of Salafism.[13] It seems clear that Khani was an important channel for the ideas that would become known as Salafi reform. But in addition to that, Khani was also the last link in a genealogy of prominent Naqshbandis whose rivalries and trials and tribulations throw light on the structure of Damascene politics throughout most of the nineteenth century.

The Naqshbandiyya was introduced into Damascus in the eighteenth century by Muhammad Murad al-Bukhari, a renowned Kurdish *'alim* and the most important propagator of the Indian and Central Asian Naqshbandiyya to the Arab world of his day. Perhaps because the Muradi family saw its interests primarily in the office of Hanafi Mufti, perhaps because the Naqshbandi order had stagnated under their distracted leadership, perhaps because it no longer enjoyed the official favor that it had in Muhammad al-Muradi's day, or perhaps for a combination of all of these reasons, Mufti Husayn al-Muradi invited Shaykh Khalid al-Naqshbandi to Damascus to take over leadership of the Naqshbandi order around 1823. Shaykh Khalid

al-Naqshbandi was one of the most influential figures in the long history of
that order, even eclipsing Muhammad al-Muradi. Like Muradi, Khalid was
a Kurdish Sufi. He had passed through Damascus in the first decade of the
nineteenth century and studied with the local Shafi'i scholars. After engag-
ing in damaging political intrigues in Baghdad and Kurdistan, he sought a
new home in Damascus under the patronage of the Muradis. A highly
charismatic figure remembered for his rigid, even intolerant, Sunnism and
several treatises, including a commentary on the *Maqamat al-Hariri,* Khalid
did indeed breathe new life into the order. As will be seen, he became a
major player in Damascus politics.

Khalid's chosen successor in running the brotherhood was an outsider,
Shaykh Muhammad al-Khani (the elder), a rigorous Qadiri Sufi shaykh
from Hama known in that town for emphasizing the duty of prayer to his
Sufi followers. It seems that in the years between 1832 and 1860, Khani
quietly led the Naqshbandi order, teaching the Sufi reformist literature of
al-Sha'rani.

The 1860 massacre left the Christian community devastated but also left
the Muslim community of Damascus reeling. With the disbanding of the
Tanzimat-era advisory council and the exile of its most prominent members, the Sunni community lost in one fell swoop its newest and oldest
political institutions—the advisory council and the Shafi'i Mufti. The
Naqshbandi order, under the continuing leadership of the Khani family,[14]
reemerged in this context as the new locus of spiritual authority in the vacuum. If the Naqshbandiyya was no longer the direct vehicle of power that
it had been in the 1820s and 1830s, it was at least a forum for the discussion of Islam's role in the new Ottoman world order. It was in the younger
Muhammad al-Khani's circle that the emergent generation of Salafi reformers like Jamal al-Din al-Qasimi met with the older generation of localist
Shafi'i *'ulama.* It was also Muhammad al-Khani who seems to have popu-
larized the works of al-Sha'rani in the period following 1860. He has the
largest collection of Sufi literature, and his estate lists the most extensive collection of al-Sha'rani's works.[15] His biographical entries list al-Sha'rani's
works as part of his education.[16]

Another factor would have strengthened the Naqshbandiyya's renewed
importance after 1860—its association with Amir 'Abd al-Qader al-Jaza'iri.
In 1855, the hugely popular leader of the Algerian resistance had come to
Damascus with his generous French pension and large entourage.[17] His
family ties with the Khanis dated back to 1825 and 1826, when 'Abd
al-Qader and his father had studied with Shaykh Khalid and the elder
Muhammad al-Khani for several months during their travels on the hajj. By

his well-known actions and protection of Christians in 1860, 'Abd al-Qader had emerged as a hero of those tragic events and as one remaining pole of old-style moral authority in the city. In 1864, the same year that he married a daughter of Shaykh Khalid, Muhammad al-Khani began to receive a stipend from 'Abd al-Qader, was made guardian of two of his daughters, and was bequeathed a substantial sum of money (*wasiya*) in 'Abd al-Qader's legacy.18 Among the relations of the Amir 'Abd al-Qader was the Shaykh Tahir al-Jaza'iri, who had collaborated closely with Midhat Pasha to start Muslim-funded schools and libraries in the reform period of the late 1870s. All the important Muslim intellectuals of the prewar period studied with him, from Jamal al-Din al-Qasimi to Muhammad Kurd 'Ali to many of the members of the decentralization group to be executed during World War I.19 Future journalists and politicians discussed Islamic historical heritage and the Arabic language and manuscripts with this key associate of the Ottoman provincial federal project.

The importance of the Khani family in the Naqshbandiyya was not that they were charismatic leaders in the style of Shaykh Khalid and the Amir 'Abd al-Qader. Instead, they were interpreters and spiritual teachers who reconciled the various trends and forces that swirled about in the aftermath of 1860. As the primary reader and teacher of al-Sha'rani in Damascus, Muhammad al-Khani would have preached the compatibility and interdependence of Sufism and *shari'a*, the equivalent status of the various legal schools, and those schools' secondary status to the *hadith* and Quran, which should be directly accessible by all educated Muslims. The issue of the equality of the legal schools was not just about Hanafi/Shafi'i competition and the relation to the Ottoman state but was also relevant to the immigration of unprecedented numbers of North African Malikis in the entourage of 'Abd al-Qader and the continuing Wahhabi presence in the southeast. More importantly, the Naqshbandi interpreters of al-Sha'rani would have stressed that the moral compass that could have guided Muslims through the past decade's difficulties was located in the dual roots of Quran and *sunna*. And as the closest Damascene to 'Abd al-Qader, Muhammad al-Khani would have played another role—that of mediating the intense mysticism of 'Abd al-Qader and his spiritual guide Muhy al-Din Ibn 'Arabi into something that the less mystically inclined could approach and appreciate, since the controversial tradition that Ibn 'Arabi represented was a potential source of stabilizing local identity. Al-Khani, with the help of al-Sha'rani, provided the basis for discussion and cooperation among the various sectors of the Islamic community.

By the end of the century, the Khalidi Naqshbandis were weakened by territorial and leadership disputes and the opening up of at least two rival branches claiming the legacy of Shaykh Khalid.[20] 'Abd al-Majid, who is remembered as a talented litterateur as well as a Sufi—and who seems to have been the most promising potential leader of Sufi/Salafi/Arabism—died in 1901 without ever taking over the branch.

By the end of the century, Islamic reformers seem to have cut their ties to Sufism and reinvented the principles of Sunni and Quranic fundamentalism as their own. Jamal al-Din al-Qasimi, for example, had been a student of Muhammad al-Khani for nearly fifteen years, but he left the Naqshbandi order shortly after his initiation.[21] Like al-Sha'rani, the Salafis scorned both mediocre jurisprudence and its practitioners and heterodox Sufism.[22] But telltale details indicating that the Naqshbandiyya's reading of al-Sha'rani was a main component of Salafism remain. Consider the so-called *"Mujtahids* Incident"* recorded by al-Qasimi and retold by Commins:

> The fifth meeting (in 1896, of what would become the Salafi inner circle) marked a step toward a sharper definition of the group's purpose. The members decided to select a book to study together, and after brief discussion, they agreed on 'Abd al-Wahhab al-Sha'rani's *Removing the Affliction from the Entire Community (Kashf al-Ghumma)*, a sixteenth-century work that compiled Prophetic oral reports setting forth the precepts of rituals and transactions. Al-Sha'rani had embraced the same position as the Salafis in opposing legal school partisanship and claiming the right to examine the proofs of legal schools' precepts. He tried to base rulings on Prophetic oral reports, which he placed above those decisions of the legal schools that were based on jurists' opinions. Qasimi undertook to compose a gloss on the work, annotating its oral reports and explaining difficult passages.

> The meeting to discuss al-Sha'rani's book was apparently infiltrated by hostile parties whom al-Qasimi does not identify, and the rumor was spread that the reading group was engaging in *ijtihad* (legal interpretation), a forbidden practice. The claim was taken to the Ottoman administrative council.

> At a meeting of the provincial administrative council, the governor asked the jurisconsult [Hanafi Mufti] Muhammad al-Manini what he

knew about the group. Manini is reported to have displayed anger at the group in order to placate the governor and to secure his post. The administrative council decided to appoint an investigative council headed by the magistrate and including the jurisconsult and his deputies. . . . On January 27, 1896, Qasimi and five other *'ulama* appeared before the special investigative committee, which had assigned Manini the task of interrogation (perhaps because the magistrate did not speak Arabic). . . . Manini [then] asked why the group studied al-Sha'rani's *Removing the Affliction* and why Qasimi wrote a gloss on it. Qasimi stated that the group simply chose a book famous for its oral reports and still used by scholars; as for the gloss, he merely wanted to define precisely a few obscure terms. The jurisconsult retorted that the group had no business studying oral reports or Quranic exegesis, and that it should restrict its study to books of jurisprudence. Manini then put on a glowering expression and said, "It has become known in Damascus that you said in answering a legal issue "Take [the decision] according to the Jamali school." Qasimi denied the charge, and after the jurisconsult berated him, he ordered that Qasimi be detained at the police station.[23]

In the end, al-Manini was intimidated by the crowds assembled to hear the outcome of the investigation. Al-Qasimi was released from jail and congratulated by Muhammad al-Khani and other shaykhs, who reassured him that the incident had improved his popular image. The Ottomans concluded that this was an academic matter that did not threaten them. Al-Qasimi made it clear that al-Manini was a weak character who was being manipulated by undisclosed others; he taunted al-Manini by saying that no one would have dared to claim that *ijtihad* was being practiced in the days of his predecessor—that is, when the post of the Hanafi Mufti still carried weight.

The link between the Naqshbandiyya-Khalidiyya and the Salafi movement was not something that came directly from the substance or practice of Khalidi Naqshbandi Sufism itself, but rather the result of the convergence of Muhammad al-Khani's interest in al-Sha'rani, the availability of the literature in accessible printed form, and the history of the Naqshbandi order in Damascus as a site for the negotiation of local rivalries and the influence of the Ottoman state.[24] This would explain why the Salafis found it so easy to renounce their ties to Sufism so completely that, until recently, most historians have been surprised to learn that there was ever a connection between them.

My records show that two of the people with the most copies of al-Sha'rani's works in their libraries were Muhammad al-Khani, the last strong head of the Khalidiyya Naqshbandiyya and al-Sha'rani's main proponent, and Muhammad Manini, the weak Hanafi Mufti in the 1890s and the Salafis' main public detractor. This is a reminder that the productive study of texts in context is not necessarily about discovering an explicit expression of the politics of the day or a program for the times, but about locating objects of contestation. The idea that books and knowledge are for thinking with, not for fetishizing, was al-Sha'rani's message to the *'ulama* of al-Azhar in the sixteenth century, and proved durable.

In this chapter, I have been arguing that al-Sha'rani provides clues for interpreting the history of nineteenth-century Damascus. Knowing what readers were reading makes it possible to make an educated guess at what religious and social issues were on their minds. That in turn allows the reinterpretation of the familiar accounts of family history, rebellions, and advisory council politics and apperception of a new underlying structure. Al-Sha'rani's works highlight a set of issues that must have had significance for the reading elite—the relationship of scholasticism and spirituality, the danger of competing legal schools, the compatibility of high mysticism with orthodoxy, the role of discipline in creating a God-graced life. At another level, by looking at book ownership (and presumably readership), a network of readers can be identified. Sociologically, this small community of readers of Sufi literature must have been very important in bridging the gap between the popular orders and educated people generally—whether high literary mystics, traditional jurists, or the small but growing and powerful class of military men and technocrats who spent their time mastering Ottoman and French and studying the civil code. Their literary Sufism moved these readers away from and above attachments to particular orders and rituals.25 The Sufi Naqshbandi culture of nineteenth-century Damascus, with its strident Sunnism, its printed literature, and its increased responsibility as one of the last bastions of religious power in a rapidly changing society, created psychological *murids* or seekers rather than *darawish,* traditional poverty-stricken ascetics.26

In the Naqshbandi Salafi story, we can see the complete transformation of one branch of Sufi practice into reformist Salafism, which subsequently concealed its own Sufi origins. Patterns of book ownership, unlike patterns related to money, remain very stable over the course of nearly half a century. The inelasticity of the reading market for al-Sha'rani's work has forced us to interpret through his work's lens changes in urban politics and development and the emergence of Islamic reform. Al-Sha'rani is unchanging, and through the constant perspective of this lens we see the changes in the city and culture. The development of some of the most radical political and religious thought that adapts principles of Westernization and Islamic activism comes directly from a deeply embedded local tradition all but invisible to European consuls. But surely there were other courses of intellectual and Islamic change.

One might start by asking why al-Qasimi and others effectively broke their links to Sufism and the Khalidiyya branch. Telltale signs of the Khalidiyya origins remain—'Abd al-Hamid Zahrawi's treatise on Sufism and *shari'a,* snippets from biographies and memoirs, and social networks—but by the twentieth century the Salafis are associated with the Egyptian decentralization movement, with journalism and publishing, with reason and the Islamic principal of *ijtihad.* In al-Qasimi we see an interest in Wahhabism, traditionally the enemy of Sufism. Admittedly, al-Qasimi dissociated himself from the most intolerant aspects of Wahhabi doctrine, namely Ibn Taymiyya's attacks on the great Damascus-based Sufi Ibn al-'Arabi and *takfir* or excommunication. The reason for the rational Khalidis' distance from the Khalidiyya bespeaks a countertrend within the movement.

As it happens, the sect's founder, Shaykh Khalid, had a younger brother who fiercely resented al-Khani's takeover of the Khalidiyya order as Khalid's Damascene deputy. Mahmud al-Sahib was no scholar—many of his writings are garbled or appear to have been written by someone else. He was a very different kind of Sufi, one who preferred ecstatic trances and defended the more traditional role of silent obedience—*dhikr* ritual rather than the *ijtihadi* version of Sufi critique that would develop among al-Khani's line. In the power struggle over the fate of the Khalidiyya order we see al-Khani (who read al-Sha'rani and married the daughter of Khalid and the Shafi'i leader al-Ghazzi's sister and produced the Salafi Khalidi line) versus Mahmud al-Sahib and his son and descendants. As'ad al-Sahib, Mahmud's son, cultivated a relationship with the Sultan 'Abdulhamid and his Aleppine advisor on Islamic affairs Abul-Huda al-Sayyadi and was granted official control over the Khalidiyya through residence in the Suleymanniya Mosque. In 1898, As'ad even succeeded in blocking 'Abd al-Majid al-Khani from taking over the Muradiyya branch of his father and grandfather, instead securing the appointment of an unqualified uncle of 'Abd al-Majid and therefore successfully monopolizing the branch.27

This is significant because the associates of Mahmud al-Sahib were among the most prominent mainstream servants of the Sultan in Islamic policy. Muhammad al-Manini, the Hanafi Mufti publicly mocked by Jamal al-Din al-Qasimi, gained his position through the intervention of al-Sahib, Abul-Huda, and the Sultan. Finally, their protégé 'Arif al-Munayyir was the chief propagandist for Sultan Abdulhamid's Hijaz Railway project. In selling the Hijaz project in the first years of the new century, 'Arif Munayyir was purveying a new practical Islam in the service of the state.[28] If the Khani literary branch of the Khalidiyya gave rise to Salafi *ijtihad,* the rival Sahib line gave rise to a practical, nonliterary practice in which traditional nonrational devotional practices and the building of the Hijaz Railway policy were both important.

7

BAB AL-WATAN:
ON POLITICAL CAPITAL,
1897–1908

As we saw under *Wali* Midhat Pasha in chapter 2, the continued development of the province of Suriyya as model federal state and as the fiscal
engine of a needy empire required greater political and economic capital
than was available locally. The new types of capital that flowed into the area
in the next generation were driven by a structural relationship instituted in
the 1880s. The huge Ottoman state debt to European creditors that had
accumulated since the 1850s and that had resulted in default in 1875 led
to the establishment of the Ottoman Public Debt Administration in 1882.
Sultan 'Abdulhamid reluctantly established the commission by decree under
pressure from the European powers whose investors had bought Ottoman
government bonds. The Public Debt Administration consisted of European
representatives who monitored and managed bond emissions and payments
and various state industries. Over time, the Public Debt Administration
became the advocate of the development of Ottoman lands in the interests
of their European constituencies.[1] Promoting capital-intensive European
investment and facilitating the granting of concessions for larger-scale projects—namely ports and railroads—became important parts of this body's
work and were seen as promoting the interests of European capital as well
as modernizing the empire.

The infrastructure projects, increasingly associated with European imperial goals, gave concrete footholds to European visions of geography (and
intra-European rivalries) in the province of Suriyya. French private capital
invested in roads, ports, and railroads challenged the autocratic Sultan
'Abdulhamid to come up with ways to protect the Ottoman state from con-

tinuing European encroachment. The ways in which the sultan sought to impose the invented traditions of a centralized Islamic Ottoman citizenship on the province through his own public works projects were a response to the reshaping of the Ottoman Empire and the aspirations of its subjects by the effective integration of the empire into Europe by debt and the planting of European stakes in the landscape.[2]

It was not until the 1890s through the eventual appointment of two key lieutenants that the city of Damascus and the surrounding provincial hinterland became the site of Hamidian projects to develop and promote a form of political Ottoman and Islamic political capital that would bind Suriyya closer to Istanbul. European capital—particularly French capital—had a head start on building infrastructure and strengthened European visions of an autonomous Ottoman Suriyya that would serve as a French foothold. By the 1890s, various French private interests had already made a series of investments in port, road, and rail building and in education. In the late 1890s, this was effectively countered by the grand project of Ottoman Islamic sovereignty and unity represented by the public Hijaz Railway. Up through the Young Turk revolution in 1908, the region around Damascus was the scene of two rival projects to reshape the transport landscape. Both invested heavily in and pumped up contrasting images of modernity inscribed on the land. Ultimately, residents of Suriyya would have two political visions from which to choose— the first, Ottoman, was a centralizing vision that depended on the legitimating effect of Islam; the second, European (particularly French), emphasized decentralization and autonomy under European tutelage and protection. These poles—the civic Ottomanism and Islamism versus the promise of European protection for autonomy—would orient the ranges of choices people could make about political identity and economic allocations.

French capital was behind the most ambitious infrastructure projects of the 1890s, namely railroad concessions for a series of lines (Damas-Hamah et Prolongements) that promised to facilitate the flow of Syrian grain to the Mediterranean coast. On the other hand, with the prompting of his second secretary for Arab affairs, the Damascene 'Izzat 'Abed Pasha, the Sultan Abdulhamid took personal interest in a competing railroad, the Hijaz Railway project. Under the leadership of Husayn Nazim Pasha, a governor as effective as Midhat but more loyal to the Sultan, this project would trump the French rail project's profitability by World War I. The scheme also served as a massive ideological and infrastructural public project that combined Islam and the economy in service to the state, a philosophy that the people and the Young Turk revolution were ready to support in 1908.

Decentralization and French Influence

French interests in securing an Eastern Mediterranean share of the "sick man of Europe" necessitated the conceptualization of a geographically distinct yet culturally and politically dependent Syria. This discourse equipped the growing circle of beneficiaries of French protection and investments with the building blocks of what would become a nationalist rhetoric of rights, collective honor, and shared history that were fundamental to Arab nationalism even after it became thoroughly anti-European. In the middle decades of the nineteenth century, French interventionism in Syria had meaningful results for Christian subjects of the Ottoman Empire and meaningful influences on the administrative structure of Lebanon and on the field of education. In the latter decades of the century, French interests were rocked by the competition between clericalism and secularism and were more sharply defined by the increasing tension of intra-European rivalries. The language of French-style autonomy gained wider circulation and application as French ambitions were transferred from the Christian groups to the land of Syria itself.

The institution of the capitulations provided for French-Syrian relations the notion of a covenant, which was central to the emergence of Arab liberal political thoughts and programs. French imperialists were adept at reiterating the terms of the agreements of capitulation to portray a glorious historical alliance. French apologists were quick to seize on how that bestowed upon France rights and paternalistic duties in Syria. French propagandists claimed that Syria was considered by France "a moral patrimony" and that France "covers the Syrian people with a maternal protection," citing the convention of 1640 signed by Louis XIV; the letters of protection for the oriental Christians renewed by Louis XV in 1737; the *firmans* of 1640 and 1751; the treaties of Paris, London, San Stefano, and Berlin; the papal circulars of 1888 and 1898; and the interventions of 1845 and 1860.[3]

The French protective mission did many things for France—it deflected clerical activity from metropolitan France and provided an outlet for that spirit; it maintained a French presence in the Levant even as high diplomacy lent support to the declining Porte in Istanbul; and, through its schools and hospitals, it was a conduit for the spread of French culture. The capitulations on which this "tradition" was based guaranteed economic advantages

and had given France a preeminent role among European countries as pro-
tector of Christianity in the *pays hors-chrétienneté*—a significant boost to
imperial techniques. After the French Revolution and again after 1881,
French clericalism was most at home abroad. With the establishment of the
Third Republic in 1881, clericalism, banished from the metropole, thrived
in the Levant. Expenditures on missions doubled between 1881 and 1884.4

French railroad projects reflected, even more than elite education, the
effective reorientation of modern Syria.5 A series of short lines connected
the major commercial centers of the interior with their Mediterranean
ports. The Société Ottomane du Chemin de fer Damas-Hama et Prolongements (DHP) completed the Damascus-to-Beirut line in 1895 and the
Hums-to-Tripoli line in 1911, and Chemin de fer de Palestine operated an
87-kilometer line from Jerusalem to Jaffa from 1892. Concessions were also
granted for a French line between Aleppo and Alexandretta. Another series
of lines from north to south ran parallel to the mountains. DHP completed a 331-kilometer line from Aleppo to Hama to Hums to Rayak in 1906;
it continued the Beirut-to-Damascus line south to Muzayrib and drew up
plans for a line from Rayak to Lydda and Lydda to Cairo. These linear
French investments—as much as the patchwork of the urban districts of
Aleppo, Beirut, and Damascus; the *sanjak* of Deir ez-Zor, the *mutessarifiyya*
of Jerusalem, and the autonomous Mt. Lebanon—efficiently sketched an
outline of the land of Syria. The port cities would give onto a French
Mediterranean and trade with the ports of the Midi. The coastal-trade view
of Syria's future provided an alternative to domination by Egypt and
increasingly an alternative to Istanbul.6

Hamidian Centralization and Practice

After his destruction of the British-sponsored reformer Midhat Pasha, the
Sultan 'Abdulhamid sought to counter growing European influence and liberalism in his realm through the promotion of non-*ijtihadi* Islam,
Ottomanization, invented traditions, censorship, and public works. This
sultanic defiance of the European bond could easily have remained a fiction
of propaganda as far as Suriyya was concerned were it not for the appearance of two key lieutenants of the sultan: a Turk posted in Damascus,
Husayn Nazim Pasha, and a Damascene posted in Istanbul, 'Izzat 'Abed
Pasha, who allowed his projects of invented tradition to be enacted in the
theater of Suriyya by the late 1890s. Nazim Pasha and 'Izzat Pasha combined the qualities of the earlier generations of reformers—creativity, self-
preservation, and control—and allowed a reprise of the public works projects of the Tanzimat period. Under their self-interested guidance, Damascus

once again became the canvas for the inscription of ideological changes on the landscape.

The career of 'Izzat 'Abed Pasha, the Damascene planner of the Hijaz Railroad, exemplifies the way in which political capital was accumulated and spent around this centralizing project. He was the sultan's second secretary and the scion of a Damascene family. After the best French and Arabic educations, he rose through the ranks of the Ottoman *mukhabarat* (secret service) until he headed both the Turkish and Arabic sections. He was secretary of the administrative council of the *wilaya* of Suriyya and head of the legal system of Suriyya and Beirut. In 1878, he edited the state newspaper *Suriyyah* and founded his own paper, *Dimashq,* both Arabist and Ottomanist in tone. After a stint as inspector general of the legal system in Salonika, he headed the criminal, appeals, and commercial and mixed courts in Istanbul. In the 1890s, he moved even closer to the Sultan when he was appointed the Sultan's Arabic secretary with rank of close associate or *qarin.* He fell from grace shortly before 'Abdulhamid's own deposition in 1908.

In the intervening fifteen years, this native of Damascus, charged with setting financial and political policy for the Arabic-speaking lands, held power that made others in the Sultan's inner circle—notably the Aleppine Abul-Huda al-Sayyadi, the Sultan's adviser on Islamic affairs—jealous. In addition to legal oversight and diplomacy, 'Izzat distinguished himself by his efficiency in public works projects. He economized on a North African telegraph project and oversaw construction of the telegraph line from Damascus to Medina, providing the lumber for posts from his own private holdings. He reportedly bested a private British plan to run a telegraph line between the Ottoman Empire and Europe, carrying it out at a fraction of the private company's proposed cost. In addition, he had set up *waqf* endowments for hospitals and orphanages in Medina, and he understood how to mobilize religious resources for social services.[7]

Husayn Nazim Pasha's rule spanned the years from 1897 to 1909, making him the longest-serving governor of the century.[8] He had enjoyed the confidence of the Sultan Abdulhamid as the minister of police in the 1890s. Prior to that influential posting, he had studied in France in the 1870s, worked as a translator in the Ministry of Public Works, and edited the official Ottoman newspaper. In 1879, he became *maktubji* (secretary) of the Istanbul municipality. His background thus combined journalism and literacy with urban administration, and he had particular expertise in public works projects. He proved to be the effective instrument of Hamidian manipulation of public space in Damascus.

During Nazim Pasha's rule in the last years of the nineteenth century, the Hamidian project took the form of new architectural façades and public works projects to resurface the city and the Hijaz Railroad to symbolize pan-Islamism, modernization, and imperial control. The new face put on Damascus formed the backdrop for Kaiser Wilhelm's 1898 visit to the city. A new town hall and a new government building (*serail*) housing all the departments of the modern provincial bureaucracy were built, and other government buildings were restored under the *wali*'s personal supervision. The Hamidiyya Barracks overlooking the Barada River, the primary facility of the Fifth Army Corps, were renovated and extended. A European-style hospital, the Mustashfa al-Hamidiyya, and a modern lunatic asylum were built to complement the military hospital dating from the Egyptian occupation.[9] The first part of what would become the University of Damascus was ordered by the Sultan's decree in 1900 and opened in 1903 after some financial pressure on Nazim Pasha. The school was intended to bypass the French and American medical schools in Beirut and the expense and distance of traveling to Istanbul for training. The move was made with a close eye on Muslim public opinion.[10]

The work of Randi Deguilhem on education in late Ottoman Syria shows that the Ottoman state school system of the late nineteenth century was an attempt to counter the advances of foreign-funded missionary schools.[11] The template of the Ottoman state schools in Damascus, particularly the famous secondary school Maktab 'Anbar founded in 1893, was French, but its content was Ottoman and Islamic, since an important aim of the Ottoman schools was to provide Muslim students with an alternative to the French and American missionary schools.[12] This resulted in considerable overlap between the Islamic scholarly class, particularly Salafis, and the state school system.[13]

Traditional markets, particularly the Suq Midhat Basha and the Suq al-Hamidiyya, were extended and promptly reroofed in metal after the fire of June 1901. These two main general markets of Damascus reflected in their names the political conditions of their founding: The one from the 1870s was named for the governor Midhat; the one from the 1890s was—like so much else from the last decade of the nineteenth century—named for the Sultan. Funds were allocated for the renovation of the Umayyad Mosque, which had been ravaged by fire in 1893 and was reopened with great fanfare in 1902. In 1902, a project of numbering all the houses in the city was completed, at least in theory. The push for government education continued, with new schools set up in a number of provincial towns.[14]

The German Alliance and Ottoman Sovereignty

*"The German inroad into Asia will remain in the
memory of Oriental nations as a troubled dream. Now
they must be awaked to the sober reality, which teaches
them that their destiny is linked with that of the English
people for a very long time to come."*

—*Dar Hayal*[15]

The Hamidian project of urban façade propaganda found an important ally
in the German Reich. Following on the principle "the enemy of my enemy
is my friend" and attempting to erect and maintain the façades of world
empire in what would prove to be death throes, the two empires colluded
into the next century in a number of failed projects and investments. But
the Kaiser's visit to Damascus in 1898 did not foreshadow this ultimately
disastrous alliance; it was a grand opportunity to show the new Damascus
to the world and to manifest the changes in local identity that had occurred
over the previous decades.

Since the accession of Wilhelm II, German imperial policy cast its eye on
Asiatic Turkey as a logical extension of its world influence. As German policy developed from the late 1880s through the end of World War I, Germany felt common cause with the beleaguered empire and served as a useful ally and mentor. The centralizing tendencies of Sultan Abdulhamid and
the Young Turks, which sought to counter French decentralizing influences,
resonated with German interests. The Kaiser's visit to Syria in 1898 and its
accompanying propaganda and Germany's growing investment in Ottoman
lands through the Baghdad Railway project anchored policy from the 1890s
to World War I.

The Kaiser's Visit to Damascus

The highpoint of Nazim Pasha's governorship of Damascus was the visit of
Kaiser Wilhelm and his empress in 1898. Although purportedly a tourist
trip, the Kaiser's visit was calculated to consolidate friendships between the
German and the Ottoman worlds. It was also Damascus's first opportunity
to present itself to the outside world. For the first time, the new streets and
roads and buildings were decked out for an outside audience. The British
consul, wary of the German leader's overtures to Ottoman officials and
public opinion, observed the whole visit very closely.

The reception of the visiting emperor allowed the city and the empire to
put on their best face. New municipal authority was mobilized for a grand

public spectacle for which "the whole city had been profusely and in some instances, tastefully decorated with German and Turkish flags in honor of the occasion."[16] The infantry kept order, and each urban community competed to excel in expressions of hospitality. The provincial government and the quarters of Damascus practiced what would eventually become their own national rituals. Flags, uniforms, parades, and fireworks had not been part of Damascus's past. While the "Emperor and Empress were met on the steps of the Serai and presented with bouquets by a deputation of young girls representing the schools of the different communities, eight of them being Moslems, two Greeks, two Greek Catholics, two Protestants and two Jewesses,"[17] the emperor made a calculated decision not to receive the more powerful representatives of minority communities or churches. These traditional protégés of France and liaisons between Europe and Syria were snubbed in a clear policy of establishing German/Turkish friendship at the governmental level.

Modern security measures became a pressing issue. The British consul wrote from Damascus of the new measures that the province and municipality were able to bring to bear for the visit. The consul wrote that

> no women will be allowed as spectators at any of the windows of these premises and that no women or children will be permitted to circulate in any of the streets through which the procession will pass. This latter measure is not only arbitrary and unjust, but absurd and it is to be hoped that the order will be rescinded as soon as the emperor is made aware of its existence. . . . I believe the authorities understand this well enough, but it having been pointed out to them that a would-be assassin would in all probability be disguised as a native of this country and in order the better to avoid detection, as a Moslem woman rather than as a man, it has been decided to take the precautionary measures above described.[18]

Even as the new security forces of the army, gendarmerie, and police were exploited, the vulnerability of rail lines was made apparent with the presence of "100 soldiers every 50 meters until the foot of the Lebanon and especially in the Bakaa Valley."[19] In the military display put on for the Kaiser, modern military inspection of the German-trained army in its drill precision best was juxtaposed with the freewheeling display techniques of a company of Bedouin warriors.

In the afternoon the emperor, attended by his suite, held a review of nearly all the troops now in Garrison here, viz. one regiment of infantry, two of cavalry, and two of artillery who after the emperor had ridden down their lines marched past His Majesty in good order and with very credible uniformity and precision of movement. To close the proceedings a body of about 150 men of the Rowala tribe of Bedoween performed what is popularly known as a "fantasia" in front of the emperor who appeared greatly interested in and amused by their manoeuvres.[20]

The Kaiser consolidated the emerging German/Turkish friendship at the personal level through the liberal distribution of honors and medals to Syrian notabilities. Relations between the emperor and Nazim Pasha were particularly warm. In fact, the success of the Kaiser's visit to Damascus was one of Nazim's most notable accomplishments as governor of the city. In spite of (and perhaps because of) the emperor's laudatory telegram to the Sultan regarding Nazim's hospitality, Nazim's efforts and successes seem to have been resented by Istanbul. Personally and locally, however, his own stock rose in connection with the emperor's appreciation and respect.[21]

With the visit of the Kaiser and Kaiserin to Damascus, the peak of Damascene tourism had arrived. This promising economic avenue was entirely dependent on an atmosphere of security and the faster and more comfortable means of transport widely available at the end of the nineteenth century. The perspective of the city that the royal visitors enjoyed was essentially a new one that had been created by tourism in the previous few decades. Rather than the alleys, gardens, markets, and mosques that described a resident's life, the royal tourists made the rounds of the mausoleums and monuments and visited the grain-wholesaling district of the Midan, which tied Damascus to the Hawran and the world grain market. They took advantage of Jabal Qasyun Mountain to luxuriate in a view of the city that until then had only been seen in passing by travelers, shepherds, and refugees. The spot where the royal entourage spent time, afterward incorporated into the urban fabric of al-Salihiyya, is still known as *mastaba,* "the emperor's seat." The new tourist itinerary around the city gave the opportunity for new commemorative tokens to be created and filled with symbolic value.

The emperor's toast at the banquet given by the city of Damascus in his honor left no room for doubt as to the aspirations for amity and support between Germany and the Ottoman Empire. It was quickly printed and circulated in Arabic in flyer form. Kaiser Wilhelm's emphasis on the inter-cultural nobility of Saladin (whose mausoleum he not only visited but also endowed), his assurance of personal and German friendship and support for the Sultan, and his equation of the sultanate of the house of Osman with the long-defunct Islamic caliphate struck a number of resonant chords in a land groping toward a national identity but riven with questions of central-ization versus decentralization and reluctant to follow the Christian minor-ity's lead toward outright dependence on France. The Kaiser's speech, deliv-ered at the official banquet in the municipality building of Damascus on evening of November 8, 1898, was effusive. He informed the gathering that "the three hundred millions [sic] of Mohammedans who scattered as they are all over the world, are united in the closest bonds with the Turkish sov-ereign in his character of Caliph might count on his [the emperor's] eternal friendship. His Majesty also referred to Sultan Saladin in terms of the high-est eulogium."22

The Hijaz Railway

If French projects and language provided the capital for decentralization, the Hijaz Railway was the Sultan's response to the French imagining of a colonial Syria and the ultimate instrument of modernizing, centralizing control. Preempting the private French lines to the coast and tying Damas-cus to the holy lands of Islam, it would be an Ottoman/Islamic public proj-ect as well as an economic and military asset. It would be the ultimate invented tradition. The Hijaz Railway project combined the distinctive aspects of 'Abdulhamid's rule—personal control, pan-Islamism, technolog-ical modernization without liberalization, Ottoman autonomy—a careful-ly planned, capital-intensive investment in the landscape of Syria.23

The building of the Hijaz Railway commencing in 1900 was the center-piece and lynchpin of Sultan 'Abdulhamid's autocracy, his focused response to the internal and external forces challenging the system he ruled. Vis-à-vis Europe, the railway would combine the best of modern technology, rival French private railroad projects, consolidate cooperation with the German ally, and demonstrate fiscal independence and autonomy from European debt. Internally, it would bind the Arabic-speaking provinces of the coast and peninsula together, sow economic prosperity and stability along its length, incorporate unruly populations, amplify and modernize powerful religious traditions and ideology, and provide a military superhighway for supplies and manpower. With a considerable amount of funding coming as religious donations from the Muslims of India, it served as a magnet for global Islam and the notion of an Ottoman caliphate.

For the province of Suriyya, the Hijaz Railway project provided another huge infrastructure project emphasizing the emergence and identity of the provincial government and state, as in Fuad and Midhat's generations, but with a critical difference. This project under way in Suriyya made the region a transit point from the metropole to the farthest fringes, tying the province to the empire. The project empowered many locally—most notably 'Izzat Pasha, the Sultan's Damascene secretary who initiated the project.

Other benefits to the economy of Suriyya and the empire were documented by Muhammad 'Arif al-Husayni al-Munayyir al-Dimashqi in a manuscript called *The Book of the Increasing and Eternal Happiness of the Hijaz Railway.*[24] In this unabashed celebration of the possibilities of the new line, this follower of the Sahib branch of the Khalidiyya pointed out that the railway connection to Medina and Mecca would increase the number of pilgrims undertaking the hajj, would facilitate governmental dispatches of men and equipment to the Arabian Peninsula; increase the opportunities for agriculture by linking potentially productive lands with markets; allow for unprecedented Bedouin industry; allow exploration and exploitation of mineral resources; and bring civilization, education, and employment opportunities to those in its path. For those whose livelihoods depended on camel transport, sales, and leasing, 'Arif had optimistic scenarios about increased intra-hajj traffic and rising volumes of pilgrims. Indeed, the project had the potential to unite religion, economy, politics, and culture in a powerful discourse of Ottoman centrality.

The benefits to 'Izzat 'Abed Pasha were highly personalized. His close relatives were granted important provincial offices. He himself received every honor the Ottoman court had to bestow, and his wealth and estates were fought over for decades after his exile. As a Syrian native who was seen as the most powerful statesman in 'Abdulhamid's realm after the Sultan himself, his memory is rather dim in his homeland. He was attacked viciously in the years after 1908 by the proponents of Arab nationalism, but this did not prevent him from being sentenced to death in absentia by Jamal Pasha in 1916.[25]

The Damascus terminal of the Hijaz Railway provided the opportunity for a new civic architecture to augment the Hamidian public spaces of the late 1890s supervised by Nazim. In 1900, the baroquely ornate Hijaz railroad station was completed. In 1907, the monumental pillar celebrating the telegraphic connection between Damascus and Medina was erected. In 1908, the tramway centered in Marjah Square was finished. Marjah became the fulcrum between the old city on the east and a strip of new European-style public buildings that stretched westward along the course of the river.

Other public works projects of the period included the 'Ayn Fijeh water distribution system (1903–1908), which would bring drinking water and hydroelectric power from the mountains west of Damascus—rendering residual the Barada and its seven tributaries, upon which Damascus had been founded.26

But even as 'Izzat designed the ultimate state project, private tramway and electricity projects sponsored by 'Izzat Pasha al-'Abed in Istanbul also marked Nazim Pasha's rule. The concession for these was held by Lebanese Druze amir Muhammad Arslan, a client of 'Izzat, but 'Izzat himself was believed to be the true concessionaire. 'Izzat Pasha first had tried to raise the estimated 60,000 Turkish pounds required for the project by selling twenty-four thousand shares of stock in a company formed to exploit the concession. When only seven thousand of these shares could be sold, however, it finally was decided to place the concession in European hands. The concession was subleased to the Belgian Compagnie Génerále de Traction, which began work in 1905. A Danish engineer supervised the purchase of lands surrounding the Suq Wadi Barada waterfalls about 30 kilometers from Damascus and a piece of land near the military hospital where the power station was to be located, the installation of turbines at the waterfalls, and their connection to the power station. This process took almost a year, and then laying of the tramway from al-Salihiyya to Qadam (outside the Midan) began.

The streetcar line was inaugurated in February 1907, and half of the one thousand new electric city lights had been put up by then. The work was largely completed in time for the Sultan's anniversary and the Young Turk coup that overtook it. All of these projects had the effect of gradually transforming the traditional urban life of the majority of the inhabitants of Damascus. In recounting them, the Damascene historian, Husni, who attributed them primarily to the initiative of Husayn Nazim Pasha, noted that under his administration "the city flourished and the spirit of civilization spread among the clans and the tribes."27

From the 1890s forward, Damascus was the site of aggressive campaigns to bolster the legitimacy of the sovereign Ottoman sultanate through showy public works projects that highlighted the Sultan's name and through building up the currency of novel Islamic practices centered on the Hijaz Railway project. Gertrude Bell noted that the "bazaar" or the Damascene Muslim middle class were effectively betting on the Sultan's successful completion of the project and thus were willing to support it.28 As Roded's work has also shown, in this time period, an increasing number of the so-called notable class were participating more and more in Ottoman education and careers.[29] On the eve of the 1908 Young Turk revolution, many Damascenes had cast their lots with the Sultan and the Hijaz Railroad, and they lived their lives in public spaces shaped by Ottoman styles. Most of the outspoken decentralizers like Muhammad Kurd 'Ali had sought refuge in Egypt, out of the way of the new orthodoxy.

A New Public Sphere

Even as mainstream support built up for the Sultan's Hijaz project, it did not preclude a widespread commitment to provincial autonomy and decentralization. 'Izzat Pasha was simultaneously the most powerful and the most disdained Damascene. The public projects of the Tanzimat reformers and public spaces sponsored by 'Abdulhamid created a powerful sense of collective selfhood. The fact that the Sultan's project drew so heavily on the Arab Islamic tradition of the Damascene pilgrimage built up a local sense of the value of the heritage that was not entirely consumed by the rail project. People were willing to acknowledge the value of the project and yet were quite happy to dispense with its author in the 1908 coup.

Even 'Izzat Pasha, whose career was made by promoting and building the infrastructure of centralization, was wise enough not to put all his eggs in one basket. The discourse of decentralization and privatization whose language was French was an attractive hedge, and when 'Abdulhamid went down, 'Izzat took a French boat to Nice, where he spent much of his last two decades. The other part of his exile was spent in Egypt, home to the decentralization movement. The period of imperial centralization created worthy targets and scapegoats for subsequent eras; 'Izzat was the Damascene proxy for the hated Sultan, and the Hijaz railroad would be the object of the Arab Revolt's tactics. Decentralization of cultural capital offered more options to more people, a lower profile, less emphasis on public performance, more private accumulation of capital, and more innovation in form.

The new dependence of the city on private foreign companies for public utilities like the Belgian-run tram and electricity company spawned new kinds of tensions, which played themselves out in the forum of public transport. In the winter of 1913, the municipality of Damascus refused to pay the electric company the contractually stated price of its services, which was claimed to be usurious, and the company turned off the power after notification in the press. The British consul wrote:

> As the crisis developed, the train protest became more sophisticated and riotous disturbances took place in the night . . . involving damage to about nine tram cars whose passengers were subjected to insult

and discomfort in two or three parts of the city, and since then a kind
of boycott has been instituted by the people against using them. [30]

Eventually, "in the Meidan quarter an omnibus enterprise is being proposed
to replace the use of trains and it is said 1200 TL of 1 pound shares have
been subscribed among the residents while though two armed policemen
accompany each car running in that quarter, scarcely any residents ever use
them."[31]

The beginning of the twentieth century in Damascus was marked by the
filling of the new public spaces with vocal popular politics. There was evidence of political participation that impressed even a British consul and a
journalistic flourishing that turned the Syrian gaze right back at Istanbul
and points west and applied the late Ottoman governmentality to the life
of Syria. In 1904, the British consul was impressed by the new level of popular interest in world affairs, particularly about the Russo-Japanese war. He
remarked that all Muslims were for Japan and Christians for Russia and that
"[t]heir thirst for the latest news is such that as an old Pacha remarked with
a grin 'they could not be more deeply interested if Turkey herself were at
war.'"[32]

The most convincing demonstration of Damascene adaptation to the
new public greeted the 1908 coup. The popular Damascus response to the
Young Turk revolution of 1908, which restored the 1876 constitution and
introduced parliamentary rule, was striking for its enthusiasm and for the
forms it took in the new public city. Clubs, public meetings, and neighborhood parties had never been seen on this scale in the city before. The British
consul reported that

> when the sudden news of . . . an immediate and complete change of
> internal policy was received here, public excitement and emotion have
> gradually increased and found expression in a fete with illuminations
> and speeches . . . attended by some 16,000 spectators. [33]

Also, "[f]ive general meetings were held in honour of the constitution, four
of which in two public gardens were attended by several thousands of spec-
tators . . . and on each occasion more than a dozen speeches were delivered
by various speakers of liberal views which were almost without exception
temperate and conducive to allay excitement."[34]

Clubs and associations like the Hurriyet (Freedom) Club were quickly
founded and, by the first week of August, "the Hurriyet Club has made
wonderful strides of progress and already numbers some 600 members."[35]

By mid-August, two weeks after the reinstatement of the constitution, the festivities continued unabated in the new public spaces of the city, which were also coursing with electricity from the newly installed tram and power lines. The consul reported, "The merry-making and feastings of the mob are even now being continued and one quarter or section of the city after another seems to be trying to outlive the last in festive decorations and nocturnal celebrations."36 Almost a month after the revolution, the mood of Damascus seems still to have been dominated by a mood of cheerful constitutionalism. Aside from the general constitutional clubs, neighborhoods and streets organized their own local discussion groups and celebrations.

By the end of that constitutional summer, the British consul was still describing the ways in which Damascenes responded to the change of their political condition and the budding development of social organizations and institutions that would reflect the new public city and its increasingly complex urban society. From the consular reports, we learn that

> more than 25 well-organized meetings were held in the different quarters of the city mostly attended by several thousands of demonstrators and spectators and hundreds of speeches were delivered all condemning autocracy as despotic and tyrannical and eulogizing liberty and constitutional government. About 2,500 pounds was spent on these festivities, and had not the notables of Damascus with the Young Turks lately recommended their cessation, they might have continued for another month or more. It is to be remarked with pleasure that all these gatherings and demonstrations were conducted most orderly without any dispute or ill feeling among those who assembled.37

Almost immediately after the constitutional celebrations had come to an end, the same forms and modes of public gathering were applied to the world politics of the day. With some prompting from the Committee for Union and Progress (CUP), Damascus responded with clear expressions of public indignation to the breakaway of Bulgaria from the empire and the annexation of Bosnia Herzegovina by Austria-Hungary. An accompanying Syrian boycott of Austrian goods continued into January 1909. Muslims and Christians alike gathered in the new public spaces of the city in civil protest as Ottoman citizens.

> A public meeting of Damascus notables and townspeople have protested against violation of the Berlin treaty vigourously but calmly. . . .

[A] general meeting was held here this day at 2:30 pm in the municipality garden attended by about 3000; the news of Bulgaria declar-
ing independence with annexation of eastern Roumelia and of Austria Hungary annexing Bosnia Herzegovina was communicated to the
public by the president of the meeting, Abdurrahman Pasha, the Haj
Muhafizi; the speakers who followed were two Moslems and two
Christians all denouncing the act of Bulgaria and Austria as aggressive
and unjustified. . . . At the end of the meeting, the president proposed
to the meeting that a protest should be communicated by telegraph
to the foreign ministers . . . and read the form of protest to be
telegraphed. . . . This meeting and its issue were suggested by the
Union and Progress Committee but the officers and the government
took no part in the demonstration. The arguments put forward were
well reasoned and accurate and no oratory of an inflammatory or bel-
licose nature was heard.38

As the clubs and associations celebrating the constitution lost steam in
the late fall and winter of 1909, the Damascus public scene gave rise to
active and critical journalism. Along with the weekly *al-'Asr al-Jadid* (The
New Era) and semiweekly *Rawdat al-Sham,* Muhammad Kurd 'Ali's liberal
monthly scientific journal *al-Muqtabas* moved from Egypt to Damascus. In
coming back to his native Damascus, Kurd 'Ali cited the "removal of pressure from reasoning minds and the spread of freedom of the press in the
Ottoman lands" and declared that under the circumstances "the land of
al-Sham is no less ready [than Egypt] for the harvesting of the fruits of science and information."39 The first volume of *al-Muqtabas* included articles
on a range of topics illustrating local enthusiasm for and appropriation of
the liberal rationalism of the Ottoman reform movement. These topics
included freedom in Syria, praise for the constitutional revolution, a critique of separatist nationalism, human rights, journalism, the printing
press, rule and representation, Islam and civil society, women's rights, ped-
agogy, childrearing practices, and a series of anti-despotic and anti-
Hamidian essays, poems, and correspondences.

The modernizing projects of the end of the Hamidian era came to a
rather abrupt halt with the Young Turk revolution. From 1908 to 1914,
projects of turkification, centralization, and consolidation of power in the
ever more hostile Arab provinces put governmental emphasis on politics
that drew Syria back in toward Istanbul rather than on continued reorganization of the Syrian land. On the eve of the war, Damascus was home to a

liberal movement expressing popular sovereignty, and France was the source of inspiration and language for imagining a nation.

But when the empire entered World War I, the destruction of the Syrian economy only intensified the conflict between Turkism and nascent Arabism. In World War I, Jamal Pasha, the Young Turk commander of the newly consolidated Ottoman Fourth Army, was the military ruler of Damascus. Damascus was the site of unprecedented inflation of Turkish paper money, scarcity of gold, and, thus, scarcity of food. Anti-Turkish feeling reached a climax with the executions of a number of nationalist leaders on May 6, 1916, in Marjah Square, thereafter known as Martyr's Square. In 1916, the markets whose metal roofs had been renovated in the 1890s were commandeered by Jamal Pasha's war effort.

8

BAB AL-HARB:
ON CAPITAL IN CRISIS,
1908–1918

In 1908, many of those Syrians who had spent the Hamidian despotism in Egypt returned triumphantly, and the re-publication of the scientific journal *al-Muqtabas* in Damascus seemed to herald a new liberal age of provincial autonomy within a constitutional imperial framework. But the next decade would be one of war and crisis, during which the channels for capital flow built up over the previous half century were disrupted. The city of Damascus was sent spinning on its axis during World War I until it found purchase and a new set of orientations between Hashemite and French domination in the postwar period. The period between 1908 and 1918 was characterized by waves of depreciation of the forms of cultural capital that had been built up over the previous decades. The loss of value of economic, social, political, and intellectual capital during this period may have critically undermined the foundations of Arab nationalism for the next century by depleting the cosmopolitanism built up over half a century and replacing it with a crude set of British-sponsored Hashemite-invented traditions. At the end of the war, contrary to what one would have suspected a generation earlier, the city of Damascus was the object and prize of warring parties rather than the source of social movement.

Three stages can be identified in the draining of cultural capital from the system built up since 1860. First, in 1908, 'Izzat al-'Abed's circle of clients fell from favor along with the Sultan, and the most direct conduit of funds and power between Istanbul and Damascus was severed. Then, after 1909, many of those Arabic-speaking provincials who had cast their lot with the new regime, published journals, and served in the Ottoman parliament and government articulated a sense of Syrian-Arab identity by protesting *tatrik* or turkification. They associated the concept with the Young Turkish Committee of Union and Progress and mounted a corollary defense of a distinct Arab identity. And finally, by the time hostilities commenced in 1914, the desperate leadership of the Committee for Union and Progress (CUP) had reinstituted a watered-down reprise of the Islamic centralization policies of the Hamidian period. This development was in jarring juxtaposition to catastrophic military, fiscal, and political mismanagement of the province, which served as military headquarters for the Ottoman Fourth Army and was headed under military rule by the Young Turk leader Jamal Pasha. By 1918, the city and its region were demoralized, depopulated of ordinary men through conscription, depopulated of potential leaders through exile and execution, and plagued by hunger and disease—ready to be reoriented in the postwar world of nation states rather than to reorient itself.

After 1908:
Decline of Hamidian Capital

Damascus showed little loyalty to the Sultan or to his Damascene deputy 'Izzat Pasha al-'Abed, who was widely perceived to have profiteered during the public works and utilities boom of the 1900s.[1] Nevertheless, their abrupt departure from the pinnacle of the empire resulted in the overnight destruction of the political capital of a formerly influential segment of Syrian society—those associated with the Hijaz Railroad project and with the policy of Hamidian pan-Islamism. With them went the positions and powers of 'Izzat's associates and a local Damascene voice at the top of the power structure. 'Izzat's relatives, who had occupied key provincial appointments, were exiled, and his considerable local wealth was confiscated by the CUP government. The most important reshuffle was the resignation of 'Abd al-Rahman Yusuf Pasha as Amir al-Hajj or the head of the pilgrim caravan. 'Izzat, whose son was married to Yusuf's sister, had had him appointed to this post at the tender age of twenty-two, and in spite of his role as the head of the traditional camel caravan, he was also a proponent of the railway project, serving on its commission and profiting in status if not also in material terms.[2]

As early as 1902, 'Izzat Pasha's enemies in Istanbul had encouraged Bedouin disruption of the line, since the direct extension of imperial control into the desert provinces would boost 'Izzat's standing with the Sultan and decrease traditional Hijazi autonomy. The Hijaz Railway had just begun running between Damascus and Medina in 1908 when the CUP leadership installed the Sharif Husayn bin 'Ali as the amir of Medina, apparently in order to have their own man with Islamic credentials keeping order on the line at a point when it could become profitable. The future leader of the Arab Revolt quickly consolidated his local power base in the Hijaz; the CUP emphasized his credentials and prophetic lineage to enhance his power at the distant southern terminal of the Hijaz line.[3] This change of power at the Medinan end of the line was thought by some to have been the deciding factor in 'Abd al-Rahman Yusuf Pasha's resignation as the Amir al-Hajj, a post he had held for decades and that his father and grandfather had held before him. The effect of the change of government and of CUP railroad policy in 1908 was to transfer the power and prestige of the Amir al-Hajj, based in Damascus, to the Sharif Husayn bin 'Ali, based in Medina. This transfer foreshadowed the reorientation of the economy, which would give sovereignty a tribal Arab flair in 1916 in the Arab Revolt.[4]

After 1909:
Decline of Ottoman Capital

By 1909 and the definitive defeat of the conservative countercoup, those who had cast their lot with the Sultan personally found that that alliance was nothing but a liability in the Young Turk era. But between 1909 and 1913, a larger group of Damascenes who had bought into the idea of an Ottoman identity that respected provincial autonomy and Arabo-Islamic prestige still comprised the bulk of the Damascus notability. For example, 'Abd al-Rahman Yusuf Pasha, who gave up the post of Amir al-Hajj, was not so tainted by his intimate associations with 'Izzat al-'Abed as to prevent him from becoming an Ottoman senator in the new parliament. Ever the savvy investor, he had hedged his bets, and as a landowner and entrepreneur was well positioned for a new liberal era. Having been the pilgrimage leader, he had enough political capital after the 1908 revolution to become a leading Arab delegate to the new parliament. His movement from the hajj line to the parliament was indicative of a general shift of emphasis. The ambitious public works projects initiated by 'Izzat Pasha and carried out by Nazim Pasha came to an abrupt end; the public sphere buzzed, however, with discourse.

In place of lucrative building contracts and dramatic changes to the urban landscape (electrification, public transport, vigorous labor markets) and journalistic timidity in the face of strict censorship[5] that had characterized the earlier Hamidian period, the later 1908–1914 period was marked by parliamentary elections, debate, journalistic reportage, and proliferating opinion and discourse about language itself—the language of education, curriculum, and bureaucracy. Events—the Libyan war of 1911, the Balkan Wars, the Zionist movement—split Arab delegates and journalists quite evenly between those who saw Arab interests as divergent from an Ottoman policy insensitive to their particular concerns in the crisis-ridden times and those who clung to Ottoman unity as a source of strength. As these issues were discussed in parliament, in the papers, and in the election campaigns, the mechanical difficulties presented by the Arabic/Turkish language barrier at a time of increased Arab integration in the political process loomed large. Many Arabic speakers complained bitterly of *tatrik* or turkification. This was not a CUP campaign to make Turks of the diverse populations of the empire. Instead, it was the effect of the end of investment and expansion of the Ottoman/Islamic campaign of the Hijaz Railway and other public works and the sudden proliferation of talk about language differences and policies that in effect highlighted proto-national differences.[6] Nevertheless, free speech in the journals of the day—*al-Muqtabas, al-Mufid, Lissan al-Hal,* and *al-Manar*—and by Arab delegates to the Ottoman parliament flourished and began to shape a discourse of Arab interests distinct within the empire. The liberalism that accompanied this parley was increasingly influential in the government, causing the embattled and increasingly authoritarian CUP leadership to stage a coup in January 1913 and to return to a program of post-Hamidian Islamicization and centralization acutely ill suited to the times.

By World War I, there existed a class of educated Syrians, largely comprising those educated in the religious schools, whose bond with France was not one of religion but of language and culture. The new point of contact between France and Syria was not the missionary activity of the religious schools but the new social forms within which the nature of the nation was debated—salons, clubs, committees, petitions. Even as France served as the traditional Ottoman mentor on reform and survival in the contemporary world, it was also the model and potential anchor for the Syrian elements seeking to break away from Istanbul.

A generation of French-speaking Syrians used French political discourse to discuss decentralization and reform and to debate the future of Syria and its relations to Europe and the Ottoman Empire. While they may have taken radically different positions along a spectrum that ranged from advocating total dependence on France to radical separatism, they used the same language and the same forums of debate. The language used by Negib Azoury to call for radical decentralization is contiguous with language of George Samne and Chekri Ghanem, who embodied the middle ground of cultural assimilation with France and compromise with the Turks, as it is with the language of the Moutran brothers of Lebanon whose right-wing Christian perspective favored outright frankification of Lebanon.[7]

French interests and influences took the form of interstate relations, protection of individuals and communities, and schools and missionary influences (and the corollary, educational exchange). A French/Syrian elite laid down a broad base for European reorientation and change in the Syrian world. While the Arab secret societies, principally the *Lamarkaziyya* (Decentralization) group, most likely did not owe the initiatives that brought them into existence and kept them afloat to anyone other than their Arabic-speaking members, it was the French consulate in Damascus to whom they disastrously turned for support in the years immediately preceding World War I, and it was the French tradition of association and the French discourse of nation that nourished them. Ultimately, French influences would dominate in twentieth-century Syria, but during the war years and until the Mandate, rivalry between British and German styles of national culture would drastically change the Syrian landscape.

After 1913:
The Perfect Storm

In 1913, the CUP leadership wrested power from the growing liberal movement within the Ottoman government and embarked on a plan of Ottoman/Islamic centralization. This plan had even less appeal to the now-self-conscious Arabic-language movement than had the earlier Hamidian project of the 1890s and 1900s. Under Jamal Pasha, during the war, Islamic projects were salvage operations run by Germans, and the crowning public works project was a military parade ground built over the ruins of houses, markets, and mosques. With the coalescence of Jamal Pasha's archaeological policy, it is possible to witness the transformation of Islamic public capital from that described in chapter 6 to an inert and useless caricature.

What took place was the degradation of Islamic capital from the living *ijtihad* tradition of the reforming Khalidi Salafis. Muhammad al-Khani's followers were deprived of their official sponsorship of the Khalidiyya in the 1890s in favor of the less intellectual Khalidiyya branch of the al-Sahib line, which favored ecstatic trances and hierarchical obedience over free-thinking *ijtihad*. Khalidi followers who rejected the reformist line, like the inarticulate Hanafi Mufti al-Manini and the Hijaz Railway propagandist 'Arif al-Munayyir, were rewarded with government positions. For nearly a decade between 1900 and 1908, the Hijaz Railway project was the centerpiece of an Islamic policy that emphasized modernizing action over interpretive thought more effectively than Abul-Huda al-Sayyadi's promotion of popular Sufi orders. But in 1908 this, too, was undermined just at its point of completion by the Young Turk revolution and the deposition of the Sultan a year later. After a five-year hiatus during which provincial public works were effectively stopped for lack of government commitment and multiple discontents found expression in new journals, parliaments, and discourse about turkification, the CUP returned to a policy of Islamic centralization in which German orientalists, rather than Islamic reformers or Arab free thinkers, played the major role. And As'ad al-Sahib, the grandson of Shaykh Khalid, demonstrated in his journal *al-Haqa'iq*—which had been established to counter the prolific writings of the Salafis and their associates— that the Sufi order was ready to put aside even the teachings of its founder Shaykh Khalid in order to serve the CUP.[8] As'ad al-Sahib was rewarded with what Muhammad Kurd 'Ali remembers as a grotesquely lavish restoration of the Sulaymaniyya mosque, where his resolutely nonreformist and ritualistic branch of the Khalidi order was lodged.[9]

The *Denkmalschutzkommando:*
Art and Archaeology in Wartime

In 1914, one of the most powerful CUP figures, naval minister Jamal Pasha, was sent to Damascus as commander of the Ottoman Fourth Army to prepare ultimately futile attacks on the Suez Canal and to preserve order in the increasingly vocal and restive Arab province.[10] Immediately upon arriving in Damascus in 1914, Jamal Pasha was presented with documents seized from the French consulate implicating the leading notables of Damascus associated with the decentralization movement. Jamal (like so many other leading Ottomans) was culturally a Francophile, yet the war had cast him as a close German military ally. Jamal Pasha had been called to become minister of public works in 1913 to help negotiate a French loan whose many conditions included halting development of the Hijaz Railway in favor of the Damas-Hama et Prolongements (DHP) line,[11] and it was in part his good relations with the French that allowed compromise on this front. But ultimately, whether in matters of railroad or in cultural matters, the French language and milieu represented opportunities for loosening the Arab provinces from Istanbul's grip. Jamal did not act on the French consulate papers until 1915 and 1916 when they were published as evidence to justify the swift execution of the leading decentralizing notables of Beirut and Damascus.

As a former minister of public works for the empire and military ruler of Istanbul, Jamal Pasha spent a great deal of energy and money on urban projects the likes of which had not been seen in Damascus since Nazim Pasha and the Hamidian period. Since they coincided with military disaster, political repression, runaway inflation, and famine, they attract particular notice.

Along with his better-known policies of repression and extermination, Jamal Pasha was engaged throughout his Syrian rule in an ambitious program of public works, urban renewal, and archaeological exploration and description.[12] While Jamal's interest in archaeology and antiquities has been duly noted, it has been treated as the personal quirk of a complex political figure or as mere apologia designed to distract the world from his ruthless policies as the military governor of Syria and commander of the Ottoman Fourth Army. I will argue here that his program of architectural and archaeological patronage was central to his attempts to re-mobilize much-depreciated Islamic capital to consolidate his control over Muslim Damascus and muster popular support for the failing empire.

Between 1914 and 1916, Jamal brought to Damascus two European urbanists. They designed a monumental boulevard, Shari' al-Nasr (Victory Boulevard) 45 meters wide and at least 650 meters long running from the Hijaz Railway Station in the west to the western entrance to the Suq al-Hamidiyya on the east. Several neighborhoods and mosques were torn down to make space for this spectacular boulevard. It ran parallel to Marjah square and the river. The buildings of civil administration stretched out along it, and it was intended to function not primarily as the thoroughfare it is today, but as a military parade ground for the Ottoman Fourth Army. In his memoirs, Jamal wrote: "I do not think that any other oriental city possesses such a beautiful boulevard as the one I laid down in Damascus." He expressed regret that the outcome of the war prevented his Swiss urbanist from designing a similar boulevard for Istanbul. In 1917, Jamal commissioned a German architect in his retinue to design a waterfall for the Hijaz Railway Station end of the boulevard. He requested

> an oriental fountain, but not a traditional Arab roofed type, which should have cascades but should not obscure the façade of the station and thus be low to the ground. It was to have lions on it, lions whose legs rested on a Turkish banner.

The plans were duly drawn out by the skeptical Germans but not built.[13]

Jamal Pasha continued the investment in monuments done by 'Abdulhamid a decade and a half earlier. Like 'Abdulhamid he built streets and monuments, and like 'Abdulhamid he experimented with promoting

Islamic values, aided by German orientalism. For 'Abdulhamid, the Hijaz Railway and the tomb of Salaheddin had been lavished with German respect and aid; for Jamal Pasha, a bizarre episode during the war helped import Islamic values that were very far from the reformist Naqshbandi principles and even from the popular practices of society.

Theodor Wiegand,[14] a German archaeologist in the service of the Ottoman Fourth Army, presents one of the most comprehensive picture of Syria during World War I. However, the strange circumstances of his work—touring Syria and supervising cartographic and architectural surveys of Damascus and other cities as the German/Ottoman cause spiraled toward its dismal conclusion—also sheds light on the way in which Jamal Pasha sought to salvage Islamic monuments as the cornerstone of a consolidation of the province in a caricature of the earlier Hamidian project.

Wiegand's explorations in southern Palestine revealed that valuable archaeological ruins were being lost to the ravages of war, and he resolved to found a Monument Protection Unit *(Denkmalschutzkommando)* on the model of a project being carried out in Belgium and northern France.[15] To further this plan, Wiegand arranged a meeting with the leader of the Turkish army, Jamal Pasha. The archaeologist and the military ruler of Syria had a successful meeting that was the beginning of a long friendship. Wiegand's concern for the preservation of antique remains fit well with Jamal's project for regaining control of Suriyya by mobilizing Islamic remnants in the landscape. Wiegand recalled his meeting with Jamal.

> Sultan Selim is Jamal's ideal and he is having the Selim Mosque in Damascus repaired with a 150,000 Mark expense. Suddenly Jamal Basha said "I would like to have all the monuments of Syria placed under special supervision and would be willing to make a large stipend available, if I could find a qualified person." Loytved said quickly "I think Herr Wiegand would be the right man for the job." I said "I am militarily under Your Excellency's command. I would be most willing to advise Your Excellency for the rest of the war." To which Jamal replied "Then I will create the post of a General Inspector of Antiquities of Syria and Palestine expressly for you and will command that you be assigned in this post to my headquarters and my personal staff. I would hope than under your leadership the Turkish and old Islamic buildings in Damascus and Aleppo would be documented, but also all other important buildings. I agreed in principle.[16]

The *Denkmalschutzkommando* was brought into being by the letter that Jamal signed for Wiegand authorizing his tour of Syria and his expenses. Wiegand requested authorization for a trip to Petra, Karak, Jarash, 'Amman, and Jerusalem before starting on the monuments of Damascus. He requested a letter granting access to all ancient ruins and monumental buildings of the country, such as mosques, churches, and schools; permission to photograph, draw, and measure them; the necessary horses, camels, camel drivers, and, if necessary, several mounted soldiers for surveillance and security; food for said animals and escort; and a first-class train pass for himself and his dragoman and third-class passes for two servants.17

Later, sharing a house in the Christian quarter of Damascus (Bab Tuma) with German fighter pilots, Wiegand and his staff began a program of documenting and restoring the local Islamic and classical buildings and ruins. The map of Damascus's alleyways produced during the war byWiegand's lieutenants Watzinger and Wulzinger is still the one used by contemporary scholars.18 It was the *Denkmalschutzkommando* that uncovered the Roman temple and market area beneath the Umayyad Mosque. They planned to issue publications about monuments discovered within the boundaries of the Ottoman Fourth Army's operations theater. The team planned a commemorative monument for the site in al-Salihiyya where Emperor Wilhelm and his entourage had camped out two decades earlier.

In spite of an economic, political, and military situation that was spiraling out of Turkish control, Jamal Pasha pursued an ambitious urban renovation project while headquartered in Damascus. Jamal Pasha's projects were not like the modernizing ones of Nazim Pasha. His grandiose view of the future was, in the now familiar nationalist way, firmly anchored in images of the past. The key to suppressing Arabism was a combination of force and not so subtle Turko-Islamic propaganda. One project particularly important to Jamal was the renovation of the Selimiyya mosque complex built in the 1550s and 1560s by the Ottoman Sultan Selim, who had conquered Egypt—as Jamal himself was hoping to do in the Suez campaigns he led against the British. German archaeologist Wiegand reports on a visit to the Selimiyya in 1916 (this may have been an extension of the lodge of the orthodox Khalidiyya in the service of the state run by As'ad al-Sahib):

Djemal Basha carries over his admiration for Sultan Selim the Conqueror of Egypt also to this Sultan's buildings in Syria. I went this morning at 9 to the Selimiye Mosque and had a look at the renovation work, for which Jamal demanded and received one hundred and fifty thousand marks from the Ministry of Awqaf in Istanbul. . . . A splendid inner courtyard full of trees, in the middle a broad basin with a fountain, all of great charm and totally neglected. . . . In front of the Mihrab sat a handsome young stone mason with curly hair and dark friendly eyes and a fine chiseled profile. I asked him where he was from and he looked sadly at us and said "Armenian, my father and my mother killed, and I sit here and work at the Mihrab of the Turks." These are indeed hard contrasts. Here an old mosque is fixed up at great expense while in [Palestine] soldiers are going in rags and 50 camels a day starve to death.[19]

Draining the Province

In contrast to Jamal's urban projects, his other policies in Damascus drained the economy and the political arena of value. Just as Hamidian cultural capital had drained from the system after 1908, the twin wartime policies of imposing paper money on the economy and executing or exiling dozens of notables associated with the decentralization movement and the French consulate severely undercut a political economy by this time closely tied to the Eastern Mediterranean coast and Europe.

At the outbreak of hostilities, the French consulate in Damascus was seized, and records of discussions between French officials and many of the city's most prominent citizens were discovered and handed over to Jamal Pasha. His response, in keeping with his policy of intimidating the population, was to round up, try, sentence, and execute or exile the accused in 1915 and 1916. Not since 1860 had such a decimation of the city's leadership taken place, and it is bitterly remembered. Jamal Pasha is known to Syrians as the Butcher (al-Saffah), and the city center of al-Marjah is remembered as Sahat al-Shuhada (the place of the martyrs.) The victims of this episode were those persons most committed to the idea of an autonomous province, but many were Ottoman functionaries and representatives in the Ottoman parliament—that is, those most capable of negotiating an Ottoman/Arab détente. 'Abd al Hamid al-Zahrawi, an Ottoman senator, to name one, had written a tract on Sufism and shari'a. The journalist Muhammad Kurd 'Ali was only spared because the French documentation revealed that he had defended the Ottoman Empire and the Arab role within it. This purge of the Damascene notability of most of those who had had talks with the French consulate would leave the remaining notability on the defensive, and it squelched any Damascene revolt against Ottoman rule. Ironically, it also wiped out any accommodation or remaining sympathy for Ottoman rule. In executing this cosmopolitan group—which represented the elites who frequented Beirut, Damascus, Istanbul, Egypt, Paris, and the coastal economy of the Mediterranean—Jamal Pasha inadvertently eliminated any French-sponsored decentralist and Ottomanist competition to the British-sponsored secessionary movement in the Hijaz, a movement that differed dramatically from that of the bourgeois urban decentralist elite.[20]

The second policy that drained and depleted capital from the wartime city was one that led to a fiscal crisis. The new wartime Syria that Wiegand's accounts described was one brought about in no small part by a change in the meaning and value of money. Prior to the war, Damascus, where metal piasters circulated, contrasted with Constantinople, where paper from the French- and British-owned Banque Impériale Ottomane (BIO) circulated and was well known to be adequately guaranteed with gold reserves. The Damascene system was fiscally conservative in comparison to those employed in other cities because of its dependence on the agricultural region of the Hawran and Jabal Druze, where gold was the standard currency and where it was traditionally weighed, not counted. The system was solid but had little elasticity, especially compared with the coastal economy centered in Beirut, which was flexible in absorbing a wide variety of currency and where, due to the absence of any central bank or regulatory presence, the arrival of one hundred passengers on a ship from France could affect the exchange rate. In 1909–1910, the expansion of the BIO and the proliferation of private European banks, such as the Banque de Salonique, the Anglo-Palestine Bank, the Deutsche-Palästina Bank, distributed credit for the importation of European products.[21]

An expanding economy in the first decade and a half of the new century had already tied the Ottoman provinces closer to Europe and caused the inflation seen earlier. World War I showed that the Ottoman Empire was incapable of maintaining a monetary system with its limited resources, its dependence on Europe, and the different textured economies of the coast and the interior. With the confiscation and hoarding of gold and the forced introduction of paper money, the Ottoman government had put into very real economic terms its lack of legitimacy and had turned the Syrian economy inside out. Credit transformed from something locally produced and distributed, to a relation of international clientage. There was no trust in the government's paper.

Like all other participants in the war, the Ottoman Empire financed the war with paper money. In September 1914, the largely French-owned Banque Impériale Ottomane, functioning in its capacity as a central bank, authorized an issue of 4,000,000 Turkish pounds. But upon the Ottoman entry of the war on the side of Germany, that bank refused any more output. Financially dependent on France and politically allied with Germany, the Ottoman Empire went into the war in a paradox. The political benefits that France had always gained by providing chronically cash-poor Istanbul with credit were canceled by the alliance system of the war. Subsequent negotiations between German and Young Turkish diplomats and finance ministers resulted in the issuance of paper money by the Dette Publique Ottoman (rather than the French- and British-owned Banque Impériale Ottomane) that were only partially covered in specie. Seven emissions were made over the course of the war (see Table 8.1).[22]

Only the first emission was based on metal, which was not deposited in the coffers of the Dette Publique in Istanbul but rather was deposited in the Reichsbank. The bills of this first emission sold at a premium to all subsequent ones. The first emission was at a premium even to BIO bills until 1920 when the Versailles Treaty devastated the German economy and made the Dette Publique emission worthless like the rest of the emissions that were never more than promises to pay in the future. The difference between the amount issued and the amount subsequently put into circulation (particularly in the first half of the war) reflected the immediate return of the bills to Germany through the large-scale sale of German imports in the Ottoman provinces.

Table 8.1
Seven Emissions of Paper Money by the Dette Publique Ottoman and Reichsbank

Emission	Date	Amount Issued	Amount in Circulation
1	3/7/1915	6,583,094	3,147,919
2	4/11/1915	16,532,524	10,342,106
3	25/8/1916	3,106,848	2,877,104
4	21/8/1916	74,845,977	74,170,922
5	22/2/1917	32,000,000	31,969,000
6	4/10/1917	32,000,000	32,000,000
7	25/9/1918	2,499,925	2,499,925
Total			**159,0006,975**

Source: Nicholas, *Questions monétaires,* p. 28.

In May of 1916, the municipality of Damascus issued a circular requiring "all small vendors, bakers, butchers, bathkeepers, vegetable dealers, cook shops, cafe keepers, barbers and grocers of all sorts who receive small change" to bring half of the money they received to the municipality, where paper money would be given in exchange. Wiegand relates that a Damascene merchant told him a circulating anecdote that even on the scaffold, a merchant would sooner hang than change a gold pound for a paper one. Nevertheless, Jamal's efforts in May 1917 to balance the gold and paper pounds were moderately successful; he threatened the leading merchant families of Damascus with ten deportations a week until the exchange rate was brought under control.[23]

The disequilibrium between paper and gold created a disequilibrium between the traditionally mercantile coast areas and cities, where the financial situation was dependent on trade, and the agricultural lands of the empire, where a drought and military confiscation of manpower during harvest threatened the grain harvest itself. A primary reason for the imbalances was that the grain-producing regions of the Hawran and Jabal Druze would accept only gold for their grain.

> A great crisis has come about since the government wants to pay for everything in paper. The peasants, however, remember the bankruptcy of 1879 when they got nothing for their paper, and here paper money is nothing but a worthless promise. The exchange rate for paper has fallen so that in Ma'an, three days ride from the Red Sea, one gold pound (100 piasters) costs 275 paper piasters. The problem cannot be overcome with force, and part of it is that the Arabs cannot read and are very suspicious of forged notes. Also they find the paper hard to store. In the beginning, Jamal Basha hanged a great number of people who contributed to the lowering of the paper exchange rate, but it got to be too much and he had to let it go.[24]

By the end of the war, a bank director in Beirut estimated that of approximately fifteen million gold pounds invested by Germany in the Syrian land during the war and two million additional pounds invested by speculators, 60 percent ended up in the Hawran bread basket, 25 percent in Damascus and Aleppo, and only 15 percent in Beirut and other coastal areas (see Table 8.2).[25]

The conditions described here took their toll on Damascus. The famine and related disease were estimated to have killed or driven out more than half of Beirut's population of 180,000 by 1916; the death toll was reported

Table 8.2
Value of Gold Pound in Paper Piasters
for Three Cities, 1916–1918

Date	Constantinople	Damascus	Beirut
November 1916	191	219	250
November 1917	597	621	714
June 1918	460	477	570

to be 70 people a day, for a total of one-quarter of the city's population in Damascus in spring 1917. George Antonius estimated that famine killed more than 350,000 in greater Syria by 1918 (as many as 500,000 by later estimates) due to poor harvests in 1915 and 1916 exacerbated by an anti-Ottoman British and French blockade of the coast. Famine spread from the coast and the mountains to Beirut and thence to Damascus.[26]

Grain Speculation

By 1918, the economic crisis had grown so acute that the grain suppliers of the Hawran refused to enter into any sales contract with any Turkish officer or bureaucrat. The Druze, in particular, preferred to sell their wheat to the British and Sharifian forces to the south, which were able to pay double the amount that available strained city resources could come up with. Unable to provision the city and the army with wheat, Jamal turned to personal profiteering, renouncing any public duty and retreating to amass a personal fortune. The practice he engaged in with major merchants was to trade high-priced grain and the exclusive right to transport and sell it in famine-struck Mt. Lebanon and Beirut from the government storehouses for cheaper grain in the Hawran.[27] This sort of trade-in-kind profiting on the price differential over space or time is explicitly forbidden in Islamic law; by 1918, though, Islam was no longer a functional system of law and justice but had become a failed element of political propaganda.

In the middle of March 1918, a wheat crisis occurred in the city of Damascus. The price of a *jift* (35 kilos) of wheat (which had cost 160–200 silver piasters) suddenly climbed to 550 silver piasters. The needs of the city had grown steadily because of the increase of refugee populations from the evacuated or threatened areas and because of the growth of the Damascus garrison. The bread for the Damascus garrison, for civil servants, gendarmes, police, schools, and orphanages, and for the families of soldiers, veterans, and prisoners of war was supplied centrally through the government. A local miller delivered the daily bread supply directly to the barracks, and the civilians provided for by the government were supplied with bread made from the leftover in kind *('ushr)* agricultural taxes of the previous year. When that surplus ran out in March, the government provisioning agency had to buy 8 to 10 tons of wheat a day. The daily need of the unprovisioned part of the population was estimated to be 35 tons. Furthermore, there was a constant and urgent demand both from the German and Austro-Hungarian forces and from Beirut and Aleppo, where the prices for wheat diverted from the Damascus market were higher in than in Damascus.

The 1918 harvest was affected by heavy rainfall, which made transport out of the Jabal Druze area impossible. Rather than sell to Damscus, the Druze preferred to sell their wheat (a store of 10,000 tons that had to last until the next harvest) to the British and Sharifian forces to the south and to caravans to Basra and Kuwait. The meager amount of wheat in the storehouses of the railroad south of Damascus was not for Damascus itself but was earmarked at that time for the Palestine front. A commission was established to centralize and consolidate wheat purchases, to regulate bakeries, and to fix the price of wheat at 450 piasters (half in gold and half in silver). Because other cities, the Hijaz campaign, and the German forces were willing to pay 560 piasters, the best efforts of the Damascus commission were in vain. The heads of the commission took gold to Dera'a on March 23, 1918, and met with the Druze chiefs to negotiate for 3 million kilos, at 400 piasters per kilo plus the cost of train transport (40 piasters per *jift).*

That spring as the English advanced on 'Amman, they offered the Druze as much as 900 piasters in gold per *jift* and scuttled the Damascus commission's deal. The commission then announced that all the grain in Damascus must be surrendered to the government. The demand yielded very little. At this point, military providers were able to buy wheat for 450 per *jift* in Damascus and 420 piasters per *jift* in Jabal Druze if the contract was with Germans. Fearing corruption and default, suppliers adamantly refused to enter into any contract with Turkish officers or bureaucrats, according to a knowledgeable German officer.

When Jamal Basha understood that German Army officers were able to procure the grain they needed on the free market, he rescinded the threat of confiscation and the price ceiling. The return of the central provisioning authorities to the market resulted in an immediate price rise to 600 piasters and to 700 piasters in three days. As the price rose beyond the means of the authorities, they bided their time and let the precious grain accumulate in the storehouses of Damascus, intending to confiscate it at a later date. At the new price level, civilians dependent on the government provisioning programs endured severe rationing, unprovisioned people went hungry, and the military waylaid wheat transports sent from Anatolia intended for the Palestine front. By autumn, the English defeat at 'Amman, their withdrawal to the West Bank of the Jordan, the promise of a good harvest, and the reigning free market conditions all contributed to the fall of wheat prices back to 350 piasters by October 4, 1918.

These circumstances permitted government officials and merchants to benefit from the price differentials in different regions through speculation. The first such contract was concluded between Jamal Basha and the merchant Sursok in Beirut. By the terms of this contract, Sursok received 1 million kilos of grain (from the government stores) at Rayak with the right to sell the grain in Lebanon or Beirut. In exchange, he was to deliver a certain amount to the army storage house on the railroad in the Hawran area. Since other grain traffic to Lebanon and Beirut was blocked, the price there was very high and was several times the current price in the Hawran. (The price per kilo reached 19 silver piasters in Beirut and 17 silver piasters in Aleppo, versus 4.5 piasters in Hawran, 4 piasters in Salt and 'Amman, 3 piasters in Katrane, and 2 piasters in Kerak.) Those prices yielded a very large profit for Sursok and probably also for Jamal Basha. That Jamal was a partner in the scheme was generally known. The advantage of the deal, as justified to outsiders, was to save the price of transport of a million kilos of grain from Rayak to the Hawran railroad station. Actually the contract was very damaging to the state treasury because it equated the higher priced grain of Rayak with the cheaper grain available in the Hawran. A series of similar arrangements followed the Jamal Basha–Sursok contract.

Jamal Basha concluded one such deal on February 4, 1918, with a trade consortium out of Tripoli, Beirut, and Damascus. The introduction to that contract stated the reason that the deal was needed: the 2 million kilos of grain in the coastal towns of Safita and Latakia could be delivered by train to neither the army nor the government. Although transportation was always expensive, the consortium had to sell the grain in Aleppo, Lebanon, and Beirut and indeed did find the necessary transport means. If the contract had come to full fruition, the revenue of the consortium would have amounted to 30 million piasters, by calculation of a sale price after transportation costs of 15 piasters per kilo. The costs would have been only 5.3 million piasters, yielding a profit of 24.7 million piasters for the consortium members and Jamal Pasha.[28]

Inventing Arab Nationalism

The decapitation of the coastal, urban, decentralization elite—including members of the Ottoman elite—was the final element of a perfect storm of inflation of cheap Islamic values and the depreciation of decades of investments in publicness, autonomy, and sovereignty. This storm left the mantle of Arab nationalism to a marginal, recently arrived movement whose stock was inflated in 1908 by the change of leadership in Istanbul—the Sharif Husayn. Nourished by the British with a constant supply of gold and matériel, sticking to the old tried-and-true techniques of camel transport and raiding tactics, the Hashemites filled the space left by Jamal Pasha's elimination of the French decentralists.[29]

British elements, unlike important factions in France and Germany, did not harbor a possessive desire for Syria. The British contribution to Syrian modernity was that much easier because it was destructive rather than constructive. Light and mobile, it focused on existing social structures rather than on the creation of new groupings and cultural discourses. One hallmark of British imperial policy was to use small tribal groups and structures, and the British continued this pattern in their relationship with the Bedouin of the Hijaz. Rather than challenging French dominance in the Levantine cities or the growing German influence on the Ottoman government and its branches, the British worked among the peripheral groups like the Druze, the Kurds, and the Bedouin in their rural and desert environs.

Supplying their local allies with capital and matériel was one of the keys to British success. Damascus and the port cities tied to it were being drained of specie and other commodities by the Ottoman Fourth Army, Jamal Pasha's wartime government, and powerful speculators, but the marginal area of the Hijaz south of Syria was brimming with weapons and gold. One of the forgotten aspects of the Hijazi Arab Revolt, which followed the rails north from Medina to Damascus, was the infusion of gold. T. E. Lawrence's chauffeur, S. C. Rolls, remembered the abundance of resources airlifted into the area:

> I dashed up to the half-open door of the great aeroplane and took a look inside the fuselage. The huge cave seemed half full of cases of heavy spare parts. . . . Everything I wanted was there, and forty cases of petrol as well.[30]

If British-provided guns, cars, and camels augmented the Bedouin tribal system for the Arab Revolt, that system was also amply lubricated with liquid capital, namely gold. Rolls, who admired his commander's ability to communicate with the Hijazi tribesmen, freely admitted that no amount of cultural sensitivity could have worked as effectively as the precious metal.

For a typical raid on the Hijaz Railway, Lawrence and Rolls packed "a large supply of gun-cotton, a week's rations and water, a case of five thousand sovereigns marked 'Commonwealth Bank of Australia,' several coils of electric cable, a battery exploder, and several other articles which had been found useful on previous demolition raids."[31] Gold was as immediately necessary to successful operations as explosives were. Rolls' special missions to the coast were to bring back for the revolt "all the gold you can carry."[32] In one mission his golden cargo was earmarked to "buy the Sakhr tribe and their corn for the attack on Dera'a"[33] the key railroad junction of both the DHP and Hijaz lines.

The rich distribution of British gold by the Sharifian leaders Husayn ibn 'Ali and his sons in formal presentations was the foundation of the monarchical Hashemite tradition. The irony of the situation was not lost on the British troops, who spent the Arab Revolt guarding the stores of gold destined for the Arabs, gold that was unavailable in any form to them. Rolls' description, colored by his dislike for the tribesmen, is worth quoting at length.

These Arabs were rich compared with us, for each man of them received two pounds a month, and if he brought his own camel he was allowed a further four pounds, but they were not so rich as they wanted to be. Their liberal wages were always paid to them in gold; they would accept no rags of paper. They loved gold so much that they seemed able to detect its presence by the sense of smell.[34]

The destruction of the Hijaz Railway by the well-provisioned and motivated Sharifian forces represented the last phase of the wartime draining of the investments of the previous decade as new values flooded into the system. The transformation of the Syrian landscape by technologies of transport can be traced through the tramway, which symbolized the modernizing ambitions of Tanzimat Ottoman governors in league with European private capital; through the railroads, which expressed the larger-scale ambitions of European powers to knit together regions and effect economic integration; and ultimately through the automobile, which as Rolls' account shows, drastically undermined the railroads and allowed the desert periphery to develop military and political significance. The first huge task for the

British troops of the Arab Army who arrived by boat from Egypt was the building of roads from the gulf to the Arabian/Syrian border.

> After rounding the point of Sinai, our steamer anchored at the head of the Gulf of Akaba, and we set about hoisting the ten heavy cars out of her hold and moving them up the beach. The only way by which we should be able to get them up to the plateau of the interior was through the pass of Itm, a narrow corridor between high rock mountains. Its sandy bottom was obstructed by great rocks which had fallen from the cliffs, and before we could hope to drive through it we had several month's hard work before us. . . .[35]
>
> In three weeks we progressed about ten miles with great exertions, and always when we looked ahead it seemed to us impossible that we could ever make a road fit for cars to pass there.[36]

The months of exertion, however, were worth the effort. The ability to quickly reach the various tribes and branches of the Arab Army was what allowed this segmented and unwieldy fighting force ultimately achieve its aims:

> [U]ntil the end of the campaign we travelled together something like twenty thousand miles. Until then he [Lawrence] had ridden the length and breadth of northern Arabia on camels, outstaying the Beduins themselves in his disregard of hunger and fatigue. But there was no comparison between [his camel] Ghazala and a Rolls-Royce in the mind of a man who, the quicker he could shoot himself from end to end of the desert like a weaver's shuttle, the better he would be pleased. He could not have controlled the Arabs by telephone, even if he had been connected with their various shifting camps. The only influence of any use at all amongst them is direct personal influence. They were widely scattered, and the nearer he could get to being everywhere at once the better it would be. There were still times when Ghazala or her sisters could be of use to him, but very largely from this time onwards the Rolls-Royce, later aided by an occasional aeroplane, took her place.[37]

On another occasion, Rolls drove one of the key tribal chiefs, 'Auda of the Howaytat Beduin, in his car. The transition from camel or horseback to automobile was handled with aplomb. The following description of a race

over the salt-flats of Jordan illustrates a number of interesting facets of the
new automotive environment: the thrill of speed, the ability to cross new
distances in unprecedented time, the momentary possibility of opening up
new paths and tracks, and the incompatibility of those new tracks with the
old water courses of the past.

> One day I drove ʿAuda of the Howeitat on a journey. He refused all
> my pressing requests that he should sit comfortably on the cushioned
> front seat, and perched himself high on some cases of gold in the
> body behind. Such was not my idea of the seat of honour for notabil-
> ities; but still it is impossible to sit in a car, at the best of times, with
> any great air of distinction, and there is no doubt that ʿAuda regard-
> ed no seat as honourable to a grown man except the back of a horse
> or a camel. He had come with us to act as guide, and he told
> Lawrence in his deep, guttural tones that he could see better from his
> perch on the gold. All his life he had lived for raiding and fighting; he
> was the greatest warrior in all the northern tribes; and now, amused
> by the unaccustomed motion of car-travelling, he permitted his hand-
> some old face to show a good-humoured smile. When the rear wheels
> suddenly dropped into a hole and jerked him violently on his perch,
> he even clapped his hands in juvenile delight and nodded to me as a
> sign of his approval of my great skill as a driver. There he sat stroking
> his beard, the man whose single harsh word was enough to raise the
> hosts of the Howeitat on both sides of the railway line and bring them
> buzzing in hundreds around the entrenchments of Maʿan.[38]

Although the transition to the railroad mentality was a hallmark of
nineteenth-century European modern consciousness, the destruction of the
Hijaz Railroad (still under construction) by armored cars and camel troops
marked the entry of the Middle East into the twentieth century. Rolls
describes a scene:

> where we indulged in yet another wild orgy of railway destruction.
> We screamed like demons as the air was rent with the roar of our
> explosions, and bits and pieces flew in all directions. One of the
> bridges had been almost completely repaired by means of wooden
> trestles, but a fierce volley from the armored cars scattered the repair
> gangs and we drove to the scene of their useless labours, and set fire
> to their handiwork.[39]

After the primary attack on the rail line, the British component of the Arab Army surveyed the scene at the important station of Ma'an. The stark incongruity of German-made and German-maintained machinery deserted in the middle of Arabia reinforced the sense of debasement of Jamal's centralizing project in the Middle East of the World War I era.

> Several engines and wagons stood on the lines, and the place contained large stores of rails sleepers, and trestles for repairing wrecked bridges. There were machine shops fitted with the latest German machinery for the repair of locomotives and rolling stock, and containing tier above tier of labelled bins, filled with every conceivable kind of spare engine part. Such a modern and well-equipped depot in the heart of the desert astonished us. It was no wonder that the enemy had held the place in force, and strained every nerve to repel all attacks on it. Yet now they seemed to have abandoned it.[40]

Damascus was the prize, and the weakened faction of 'Abd al-Qader al-Jaza'iri was swept aside as Faisal ibn Husayn became the face of the Arab nation. The power and capital vacuum in Damascus had allowed a previously marginal element—the Hashemites—to become a weak foundation of future national thought and action throughout the Arabic-speaking provinces of the erstwhile Ottoman realm.

9

CONCLUSION

Focusing on values in Damascene society and concentrating on the movement of those values rather than on their fixed positions and essential qualities have provided a sense of the history of different spaces—families, public spaces, landscapes—at the end of the long nineteenth century.[1] The spaces were transformed as people maneuvered to make the most of the cultural capital that flowed through their lives. Many people had little capital, a few had a lot; and in times of change, all actors made choices about which vehicles provided the most security and opportunity and the least risk for the future. The way that the many and the few made choices and evaluated each others' choices affected the shape of the system they inhabited.

The transformation of modernity began as increased financial liquidity opened up competing routes from inland to coast. That liquidity went into expanding the city's residential areas outside the city walls, stratifying its markets into segments, and turning stratification into class, upsetting traditional relations of bond and labor relations. In the countryside, turning grain into a cash export crop caused social upheaval among the peasantry. In the reproduction of people through families, the new liquidity caused wealth stratification to turn into class—and made a middle class at that— as newly rich men acquired the daughters of old prestigious families. Liquidity had little effect on intellectual capital except perhaps to increase the value of traditional religious knowledge that became a lens through which to view and interpret change, one that created a Salafi Naqshbandi reformist strain of Islam as distinguished from a popular, orthodox strain that sought state favor. These local issues took place as political capital from Istanbul in the hands of governor entrepreneurs reorganized the province around Damascus into the province of Suriyya. Reformist governors from Fuad to Midhat (1860–1880) sought to rationalize, homogenize, domesticate, and control the area through campaigns of public safety, public sphere, and public space, in effect creating the environment for the expanding liberal middle class to debate, declaim, and get a sense of itself. By the late 1890s, that new public sphere was the target of Sultan 'Abdulhamid's propaganda efforts centering on the Hijaz Railway, whose construction was an ideological tour de force combining religion, economy, and cultural politics. It stood in stark contrast to the prevailing trend of French-flavored decentralization—even its architect 'Izzat Pasha hedged his bets by maintaining links to France and British Egypt. After 1908, when the decentralizing, provincial autonomous tendencies of the Damascus population manifested themselves, the depreciation of Hamidian cultural capital led to sharp reversals in the political marketplace. CUP leader Jamal Pasha reprised 'Abdulhamid's techniques of centralization through public works and Islamisation, pushing outside values into the system while simultaneously enforcing policies that led to gold flight, grain hoarding, runaway inflation, and starvation in the Fourth Army Zone. This draining of value from the system of Suriyya, tied by half a century of change to the coastal economy of the Mediterranean, resulted in the empowerment of its southern hinterland, and the invention of the public face of Arab nationalism as tied to Bedouins, Islam, and Hashemites was strangely ineffective for the next century.

Edward LiPuma and Benjamin Lee have used the concept of a culture of circulation to describe the contours of the contemporary moment of globalization. They write:

> Cultures of circulation are created and animated by the cultural forms which circulate through them. . . . The circulation of these forms— whether the novels and newspapers of the imagined community or the equity based derivatives and currency swaps of the modern market—always presupposes the existence of their respective interpretive communities. . . .[2]

Investigation of circulation trajectories has applications beyond evoking postmodern complexity. Recreating processes and constellations of circulation can help recreate the dynamics of societies large and small, modern and premodern, distant and familiar. If circulation constitutes societies through exchange relationships, can culture perhaps be the apparent naturalization of stable historical relationships between and among parties to and objects of exchange?

Whether the values in question are as basic and few as cattle and daughters or as complexly constructed (and crowded and obscured by other rival value forms) as equity-based derivatives, the pathways they travel in exchange or accumulation shape an open-ended social and cultural environment. The trajectory of any single value form provides one line—a single element of a complex matrix. The full potential of circulation to reveal culture more completely involves identifying as many forms of cultural capital as possible and beginning to identify the relationships between them. A satisfactory static model of culture and society would be a topographical map reflecting the dynamics of the relevant forms—from offspring to gold to real estate to novels to derivatives. A dynamic model of culture would include an understanding of how some agents manipulate and transform capital forms at key points in the site to manage risk and how many others are trapped in topographical structures that leave them exposed to the (supply-shock) risks of a particular mode of reproduction.

This examination of value history in Damascus suggests a few "best practices" for theorizing history as changes in value flow through a place.

1. Macro and micro, public and private, centralization and decentralization must be considered in the same context even, and especially, if this challenges disciplinary or subdisciplinary boundaries between political and social histories.
2. Purposeful action and cumulative activity, the movement of sovereign entities and the gradual unpurposeful movement of market trends, must be considered together to understand the possibility of agency within structure and the limitations of structure on agency.
3. Systems are open—studies of colonialism show that the most interesting transformations are set in motion by impacts and by economic pressures beyond the immediate locale. Traditional ethnography, which begins with a bounded group as the premise of the study, produces accounts of stasis.
4. The most meaningful change is inscribed in local, environmental terms as changes in family, residence, class, public sphere structures, and institutions. To the extent that academic gravitation toward the study of texts obscures the investigation of less tangible and familiar residues of change, it presents distorted views of change.
5. More complete models of social change are the result of all these factors taken together.

The original formulation by Albert Hourani of the politics of notables a generation ago provides the basis for a theory of agency that correlates to cultural capital topographic structuralism. In 1968, he wrote:

> The concept of a "notable," as we shall use it, is a political and not a sociological one. We mean by it those who can play a certain political role as intermediaries between government and people and—with certain limits—as leaders of the urban population.[3]

Subsequent attempts to analyze Damascene notability sociologically, namely Schilcher's *Families in Politics* and Khoury's *Urban Notables and Arab Nationalism,*[4] became benchmarks of the fields of social and political history in the Weberian tradition, but they failed as explanatory typologies. As Hourani pointed out, the value lies not in who is considered a notable, but in how skillfully a notable manages the cultural capital he acquires (religious, military, or economic).

> The two aspects of a notable's power are of course closely connected with each other. It is because he has access to authority that he can act as a leader, and it is because he has a separate power of his own in society that authority needs him and must give him access.[5]

The interesting historical actors are those who can mediate between state and society, between private and public. They can centralize while decentralizing, turn local values into imperial values and vice versa, and control enough capital fuel to jump from one set of flows to another, from one language to another. To the extent that we look only at certain families and expect religious, military, and economic power to be handed down straight from father to son, we ignore the changing forms and textures of cultural capital that empower new actors, the hoarding and failure to diversify that results in the risk of obsolescence, and the potential for change in the lateral and obscured rhythm of marriage recombination and the lowest level of differentiation of sibling rivalry.

In any dynamic system, the types, scales, and directions of cultural capital flows change over time. New kinds of actors will be empowered by them. Recent research suggests that by the beginning of the twentieth century, bourgeois values of education and national sentiment best equipped one for social mobility and influence.

NOTES

Chapter One

1   One rich and ambitious work, Keith Watenpaugh's *Being Modern in the Middle East: Revolution, Nationalism, Colonialism and the Arab Middle Class* (Princeton, N.J.: Princeton University Press, 2006), appears to reduce modernity to the practices of a middle class whose defining feature is, somewhat tautologically, modernity itself. Another important work, Christa Salamandra's *A New Old Damascus: Authenticity and Distinction in Urban Syria* (Bloomington: Indiana University Press, 2005) sees modernity as characterized by the commodification of authenticity and tradition. Both very useful contributions capture part of the complex of modernity but contribute unintentionally to the oversimplification of what they characterize as non-Western modernity.

2   C. A. Bayly and Leila Fawaz, "Introduction: The Connected World of Empires," in Leila Tarazi Fawaz and C. A. Bayly (eds.), *Modernity and Culture from the Mediterranean to the Indian Ocean* (New York: Columbia University Press, 2002), 1. This more successful approximation of modernity comes in the context of an edited volume focusing on a number of systems, but the plurality applies equally well to a single system.

3   William Roe Polk and Richard L. Chambers, eds., *Beginnings of Modernization in the Middle East: The Nineteenth Century* (Chicago: University of Chicago Press, 1968), 427.

4   George Antonius, *The Arab Awakening: The Story of the Arab National Movement* (New York: G. P. Putnam's Sons, 1946), 471.

5   Muhammad Sa'id al-Qasimi, Jamal al-Din al-Qasimi, and Khalil al-'Azm, *Qamus al-Sina'at al-Shamiyya* (Paris: Mouton, 1960).

6   Ibid., 465.

7   Abdul-Karim Rafeq, "Damascus and the Pilgrim Caravan," in *Modernity and Culture: From the Mediterranean to the Indian Ocean,* ed. Leila Tarazi Fawaz and C. A. Bayly (New York: Columbia University Press, 2002), 130–43.

8   Al-Qasimi, *Qamus,* 88.

9   Ibid., 123.

10   See Muhammad Jamil al-Shatti, *Rawdat al-Bashar fi A'yan Dimashq fi al-Qarn al-Thalith 'Ashar* (Damascus: Dar al-Basha'ir, 1994), for example.

11   Henri Lefebvre, *The Production of Space* (Oxford: Blackwell, 1991), 454.

12   Ibid.

13   See, for example, Edward LiPuma and Benjamin Lee, *Financial Derivatives and the Globalization of Risk* (Durham, N.C., and London: Duke University Press, 2004).

14   Pierre Bourdieu, *Outline of a Theory of Practice* (Cambridge, UK: Cambridge University Press, 1977), 248.

15   Ibn Khaldun, *The Muqaddimah: An Introduction to History,* trans. Franz Rosenthal (New York: Pantheon, 1958).

16   James Ferguson, "The Cultural Topography of Wealth: Commodity Paths and the Structure of Property in Rural Lesotho," *American Anthropologist* 94, no. 1 (1992): 55–73.

17   Ibid.

18   Stephen Sheehi, *Foundations of Modern Arab Identity* (Gainesville: University Press of Florida, 2004), 235.

Chapter Two

1   Kamal Salibi, "The 1860 Upheaval in Damascus as Seen by al-Sayyid Muhammad Abu'l-Su'ud al-Hasibi, Notable and Later Naqib al-Ashraf of the City," in *Beginnings of Modernization in the Middle East: The Nineteenth Century*, ed. William Roe Polk and Richard L. Chambers (Chicago: University of Chicago Press, 1968), 185–205. See also Leila Fawaz, *An Occasion for War: Civil Conflict in Lebanon and Damascus in 1860* (New York: I.B. Tauris, 1994); Abdul-Karim Rafeq, "New Light on the 1860 Riots in Damascus," *Welt des Islams* 28 (1988): 412–30.

2   See Khaled Fahmy, *All the Pasha's Men* (Cambridge, UK: Cambridge University Press, 1997), 47–55.

3   Abdul-Karim Rafeq, *The Province of Damascus* (Beirut: Khayats, 1966), 4–6; Moshe Ma'oz, *Ottoman Reform in Syria and Palestine 1840–1861* (Oxford, UK: Clarendon, 1968).

4   Foucault provides a term that is useful in evading the concept of modernization: governmentality (also called governmental rationality). It reorients the quest for development of the state itself to the practices of government and suggests that new techniques of organization, domination, and government by actors seeking to maximize their political strength were the generators of the new (modern) state. See Colin Gordon, "Governmental Rationality: An Introduction," and Michel Foucault, "Governmentality," in Graham Burchell, Colin Gordon, and Peter Miller, eds., *The Foucault Effect: Studies in Governmentality* (London: Harvester Wheatsheaf, 1991). For application to the governors of Damascus, see Leila Hudson, "Late Ottoman Damascus: Investments in Public Space and the Emergence of Popular Sovereignty," *Critique: Critical Middle Eastern Studies* 15, no. 2 (2006): 151–69.

5   See Stefan Weber, "Der Marja-Platz in Damaskus: Entstehung Eines Modernen Stadtzentrums Unter den Osmanen als Ausdruck Einen Strukturellen Wandels," *Damaszener Mitteilungen* 10 (1998): 291–344.

6   Ibid.

7   James Lewis Farley, *Turkey* (London: S. Low, Son and Marston, 1866), 40.

8   See Max L. Gross, "Ottoman Rule in the Province of Damascus 1860–1909" (PhD diss., Georgetown University, 1979), 34; British Foreign Office 78/1586 (FO 78/1586) Damascus, Rogers to Bulwer, no. 48, November 30, 1861. Also Roderic Davison, *Reform in the Ottoman Empire 1856–1876* (Princeton, N.J.: Princeton University Press, 1963), 88–93; Bernard Lewis, *The Emergence of Modern Turkey* (Oxford, UK: Oxford University Press, 1968), 117–18.

9   Fawaz, *An Occasion for War,* 101–05 and 112–31.

10   Ibid.

11   Gross, "Ottoman Rule," 82–83.

12   Lady Anne Blunt, *Bedouin Tribes of the Euphrates* (Whitefish, Mont.: Kessinger Publishing, 2006), 371–72 (originally published in New York in 1879); Gross, "Ottoman Rule," 70–79. For more information on particular politics of Bedouin tribes in the nineteenth century, see N. Lewis, "The Frontier of Settlement in Syria 1880–1950," *International Affairs* 31 (1955): 50. The eighteenth-century rise of the Wahhabi movement in Arabia disrupted the traditional migration patterns of the larger tribes (the Shammar and the 'Anaza) and their subgroups and dependents, and these tribes' new migration patterns had a devastating effect on the villages and towns of the Damascus countryside. See also FO 78/1876 Damascus, no. 5, January 26, 1865.

13   See FO 78/1586 Damascus, no. 32, July 10, 1861, for details about the Bedouin/Druze alliance in the Hawran. See also FO 78/1751 Damascus, no. 50, September 25, 1863.

14   See FO 78/1586 Damascus, no. 3, January 24, 1861, on military policy around the Laja'. Also FO 78/1751 Damascus, no. 31, June 12, 1863; no. 42, August 19, 1863; and no. 52, October 2, 1863. On the capture of various outlaws, see FO 78/1670 Damascus, no. 17, July 10, 1862, and FO 78/1586 Damascus, no. 44, November 10, 1861. Also FO 78/1815 Damascus, no. 5, November 21, 1864, and Gross, "Ottoman Rule," 90–91.

15   FO 78/1829 Damascus, no. 24, June 21, 1864.

16   FO 78/1876 Damascus, no. 5, January 26, 1865, enclosure "Trade Report from Damascus, 1864."

17 During Rushdi Pasha's tenure, most of the reform effort was focused on details of reorganization. According to European observers, Rushdi Pasha did not share the overarching vision of the law's author, Midhat Pasha, and was only able to make slow progress on the steps of reorganization. FO 78/1876 Bludan, August 16, 1865, and FO 78/1872 Damascus, no. 15, November 21, 1865.

18 FO 78/1872 Beirut, no. 31, November 11, 1865.

19 Muhammad Husni, *Kitab Muntakhabat al-Tawarikh li Dimashq*, ed. Kamal Salibi, 3 vols. (Beirut, 1979), 265ff.

20 Husni, *Muntakhabat*, 269.

21 Ibid., 270.

22 FO 78/2036 Damascus, no. 12, September 28, 1868.

23 FO 78/1978, no. 77, December 21, 1867, and Gross, "Ottoman Rule," 135ff.

24 FO 78/2051 Damascus, no. 9, February 3, 1868.

25 FO 78/1978 Damascus, no. 26, May 3, 1867.

26 FO 78/1978 Damascus, no. 51, July 21, 1867; no. 66, September 24, 1867.

27 FO 78/2103 Damascus, no. 5, April 10, 1869; no. 11, July 16, 1869; no. 20, October 29, 1869.

28 The conflict between Burton and Rashid was summarized thus by Ambassador Elliot: "Burton did not understand that the days when Governors General trembled before Consular Dragomans had passed—never, it is hoped, to return. The struggle for direct influence or domination among the different foreign Representatives, which was carried on throughout the Empire previous to the Crimean War, has since that time been dropped by a tacit understanding, and no Governor General would submit to the subserviency of a Consul which was common twenty years ago. Captain Burton fell into the error of endeavoring to recover for himself and for his Dragomans a position neither aimed at by his colleagues nor compatible with the altered state of affairs, and he naturally encountered the strenuous opposition of the Governor General." FO 78/2259 Therapia, no. 117, September 9, 1871, cited in Gross, "Ottoman Rule," 161, note 120.

29 FO 78/2103 Damascus, no. 13, September 27, 1869.

30 Ali Haydar Mithat, *The Life of Midhat Pasha* (New York: Arno Press, 1973), 175.

31   For text see Ahmad Klican Wasif, efendi, *Son Altesse Midhat-Pacha, Grand Vizir* (Paris: Société Anonyme de l'Imprimerie Kugelmann, 1909), 161–68.

32   Shimon Shamir, "The Modernization of Syria: Problems and Solutions in the Early Period of Abdulhamid," in William Polk and Richard Chambers, eds., *The Beginnings of Modernization in the Middle East: The Nineteenth Century,* 351–83.

33   Shamir, "Modernization of Syria," 364–65.

34   Ibid., 362; Najib Saliba, "The Achievements of Midhat Pasha as Governor of the Province of Syria 1878–1880," *International Journal of Middle East Studies* no. 9 (1978): 307–23; Gross, "Ottoman Rule," 262–63; FO 78/2850 Damascus, Jago to Layard, no. 15, December 22, 1878, and no. 17, December 31, 1878; FO 78/2985 Damascus, Jago to Malet, no. 13, April 14, 1879, "Observations on Midhat Pasha and his Power to Effect Reforms."

35   FO 79/2850 Damascus, no. 17, December 31, 1878; and Shamir, "Modernization of Syria," 364–65.

36   FO 78/2985 Beirut, no. 27, March 15, 1879, and FO 78/3130 Beirut, no. 42, May 31, 1879.

37   FO 78/2989 Beirut, no. 7, January 18, 1879; Tripoli, no. 5, September 1, 1879.

38   Shamir, "Modernization of Syria," 375; Saliba, "Achievements," 320–22, on educational and cultural matters.

39   Midhat had devoted much time and energy to the reorganization of the gendarmerie or *zabtiyya.* He recruited new members with attractive salary offers. He divided the provincial gendarmerie into two divisions. One was under the direct control of the ministry of police in Istanbul; the other was subordinate to the governor himself. The function of this latter force of 160 men, which became known as Midhat's private police force, was to spy on his opponents in Damascus and throughout the province. The new recruits for this elite force had to have working knowledge of the Ottoman penal code and rules of evidence and had to be fluent in both Arabic and Turkish. A full third of the force were Syrian Christians and Jews. The larger division of two thousand men was a patrol rather than an investigative force. Under Midhat's recruitment policy, this descendent of the Kurdish militialike gangs became less exclusively Kurdish and included many Christians and some Jews as well as Sunni Muslims.

40   Gross, "Ottoman Rule," 295ff; FO 78/2985 Damascus, Jago to Layard, nos. 25–31, October 22, 1879–November 22, 1879, and

especially the enclosure "Memorandum on the Recent Troubles in the Hawran." See also Muhammed Kurd 'Ali, *Khitat al-Sham,* vol. 3 (Damascus: Matba'at al Taraqqi, 1950), 102–3; Mithat, *Life of Midhat Pasha,* 183–90; and Shimon Shamir, "Midhat Pasha and the Anti-Turkish Agitation in Syria," *Middle East Studies,* 10, no. 2 (1974): 173–74.

41 Foucault's sketchy framework of governmentality was designed to encompass "strategic reversibility"—that is, to account for practices and even institutions of resistance at the same time as practices and institutions of government and the state. Gordon, "Governmental Rationality," 4.

42 FO 618/3 Quarterly Report Damascus (draft), October–December 1902.

43 FO 371/1263 Damascus, no. 80, September 28, 1900.

44 FO 618/3, "Memo on the Difficulties of Conscription," June 4, 1908.

45 This work, due to the source material and the importance of Islam as a currency of cultural capital, does not address the role and internal transformation of the non-Muslim communities of Damascus, which form a significant minority. For this topic, see Butrus Abu Manneh, "The Christians between Ottomanism and Syrian Nationalism: The Ideas of Butrus al-Bustani," *International Journal of Middle Eastern Studies* 11 (1980): 287–304. See Fruma Zachs, *The Making of a Syrian Identity: Intellectuals and Merchants in Nineteenth Century Beirut* (Leiden: Brill, 2005) for a discussion of the trajectory of coastal and mountain Christians who led those of the interior toward nationalism.

Chapter Three

1   W. Frawley, G. Piatetsky-Shapiro, and C. Matheus, "Knowledge Discovery in Databases: An Overview," *AI Magazine,* Fall 1992, 213–28.

2   The main *qassam* of Damascus seems to have been a subsection of the main court, the Mahkamat al-Bab, and appears to have served most of the quarters of Damascus, even those that had their own courts, until the end of the nineteenth century. Only the Midan court, serving the long southern suburb that linked the city with its agricultural hinterland, seems to have had its own *qassam,* based on three volumes and the absence of Midan entries in general in the entire sample from 1300–1310. For the period from 1300 to 1345 A.H., there are approximately eight hundred *sijills* or registers produced by the Damascus courts.

3   Abdul-Karim Rafeq, "Registers of Succession and Their Importance for Socio-Economic History," in *Actes du VIIe Congrès du CIEPO* (Ankara: Turk Tarih Kurumu Basimevi, 1994), 9–32.

4   *Markaz lil Watha'iq al-Tarikhiyya (MWT)* Law Court Registers (LCR), Damascus Series 1263: frontispiece.

5   *MWT* LCR Damascus Series 926/23 13 Rabi II 1309. The following quotes are also from this register and case unless otherwise specified.

6   Family names can give some information as to the origins of a family line, but not much else. Whether the surname indicating foreign origin is historically accurate or just a nickname, whether the immigrant ancestor arrived two or twenty generations ago, is impossible to tell from this data alone. Nevertheless, a count of the number of surnames indicating foreign origins indicates that from 1330 to 1340, 23 percent of the sample have family names indicating non-Damascene origin. The most common geographical family name between 1330 and 1340, represented in 2 percent of the sample, was Halabi (Aleppine), followed by Istanihli (Istanbuli) with more than 1 percent of the sample and Hamawi (Hama native), also with 1 percent. Seven individu-

als in the survey carried the surname of Kurdi (Kurd), seven were called Jarkassi (Circassian), five had the name Dyarbekirli (from Dyarbekir in Anatolia), four were identified as Zinji (African black), and four had the family name Tarabulsi (from Tripoli). All in all, most foreign place names indicate a Turkish origin. Other family names indicate Syrian, Lebanese, and Palestinian as well as a few Iraqi, Hijazi, and Bosnian place names.

7   Hajja, the female equivalent of Hajj, is used to designate the very few women in this time period who had completed the pilgrimage to the Mecca. The designation Hajja was almost never used, indicating that few local women went on the pilgrimage.

8   Martin Hartmann, *Reisebriefe Aus Syrien* (Berlin: Dietrich Reimer, 1913), 11. Also see Zouhair Ghazzal, *L'Economie politique de Damas* (Damascus: Institut français des études arabes à Damas [IFEAD], 1992).

9   See Muhammad Sa'id al-Ustuwani, *Mashahid wa Ahdath Dimash-qiyya fi Muntasaf al-Qarn al-Tasi 'Ashar* (Damascus: A. al-Ustuwani, 1993).

10 This does not include the Midan, which seems to be the only area of the city that had a separate, functioning regional court at the end of the nineteenth century and therefore is not represented in my sample. The Midan was probably at least as large as al-Salihiyya at the time. See Brigitte Marino, "Le faubourg du Midan à Damas à l'epoque ottomane: espace urbain, société, et habitat (1742–1830)" (Damascus: IFEAD, 1997).

11 Abd al Razzaq Moaz, "Domestic Architecture in Late Ottoman Damascus," in *Art turc: 10e Congrès international d'art turc* (Geneve: Fondation Max Berchem), 489–93. This resource tells us that some of the most prominent notable families from different quarters of the inner city, for example, like the 'Abed and Yusuf families, moved to Suwayqat Saruja on the threshold of the new Salihiyya and just behind the new town center of the Marja.

12 Stefan Weber, "Ottoman Damascus of the 19th Century: Artistic and Urban Development as an Expression of Changing Times," in *Art turc: 10e Congrès international d'art turc* (Geneve: Fondation Max Berchem), 731–36.

13 The formula *tabi' lil-dawla al-'uzma al-'uthmaniyya* (belonging to the great Ottoman state) began to be appended to the names of persons

mentioned in the document. Its use is irregular and depends largely on the court scribe, but it dates from a decree from 1858 at the time of the reform in the Ottoman land code.

14   See, for example, *MWT* LCR Damascus Series 1226/1; 1435/1; 1435/59; 1435/101; 1435/144; 1508/27; 1508/59; 1508/80; 1508/83; 1468/86; 1468/104.

Chapter Four

1   For background see Abdul-Karim Rafeq, "The Impact of Europe on a Traditional Economy: The Case of Damascus, 1840–1870," in *Economie et sociétés dans l'empire ottoman (fin du XVIIIe-debut du Xxe siècle)*, ed. J. L. Bacque-Grammont and P. Dumont (Paris: CNRS, 1983), 419–32.

2   Ingeborg Huhn, *Der Orientalist Johann Gottfried Wetzstein als Preussischer Konsul in Damaskus (1841–1861) dargestellt nach seinem hinterlassenen Papieren* (Berlin: K. Schwartz, 1989).

3   Abdul-Karim Rafeq, "Damascus and the Pilgrim Caravan," in *Modernity and Culture: From the Mediterranean to the Indian Ocean*, ed. Leila Tarazi Fawaz and C. A. Bayly (New York: Columbia University Press, 2002), 130–43.

4   Nu'man Qasatli, *Al-Rawdat al-Ghina fi Dimashq al-Fayha* (Beirut: Dar al-Raid al-'Arabi, 1982).

5   Colette Establet and Jean Paul Pascual, *Ultime voyage pour la Mecque: Les inventaires après décès de pèlerins morts à Damas vers 1700* (Damas: IFEAD, 1998).

6   Isabel Burton, *The Inner Life of Syria, Palestine and the Holy Land* (London: H. S. King and Co., 1875).

7   See also Jacob Landau, *The Hejaz Railway and the Muslim Pilgrimage* (Detroit, Mich.: Wayne State University Press, 1971), 71–81, for Muhammad 'Arif al-Husayni al-Munayyir al-Dimashqi's description of the Damascene hajj circa 1900 in his work "The Book of Increasing and Eternal Happiness—The Hijaz Railway" (*al-Sa'ada al-Namia al-Abadiyya fi al-Sikka al-Hijaziyya al-Hadidiyya*).

8   For an exhaustive study of the dynamics of the Midan, albeit in an earlier period than discussed here, see Brigitte Marino, *Le Faubourg du Midan à Damas à l'époque ottomane: espace urbain, société et habitat: 1742–1830* (Damascus: IFEAD, 1997).

9   Charles Issawi, *An Economic History of the Middle East and North Africa* (New York: Columbia, 1982).

10   Ibid., 53. See also R. Tresse, "Histoire de la route de Beyrouth a Damas (1857–1892)," *La Géographie* 66 (1936).

11   Zouhair Ghazzal, *L'économie politique de Damas Durant le XIXème Siècle: structures traditionelles et capitalisme* (Damascus: Institut français des études arabes à Damas, 1993). On the questions of pre-war bimetallism, inflation, and currency circulation, see Sevket Pamuk, *A Monetary History of the Ottoman Empire* (Cambridge, UK: Cambridge University Press, 2000), 206ff. For a view on late nineteenth century prosperity, see O. Okyar, "A New Look at the Problem of Economic Growth in the Ottoman Empire, 1800–1914," *Journal of European Economic History* 16 (1987). And Sevket Pamuk, *The Ottoman Empire and European Capitalism 1820–1913: Trade, Investment and Production* (Cambridge, UK: Cambridge University Press, 1987). Muhammad Sa'id Qasimi, *Qamus Al-Sina'at Al Shamiyya* (Paris: Mouton and Co., 1960). Ilyas Qoudsi, "*Nubdha Tarikhiyya Fi Al Hiraf Al-Dimashqiyya* (Notice sur les Corporations de Damas)," in *Actes du Vième Congres Des Orientalistes* (Leiden: Carlo Landberg, 1885). Louis Massignon, "Le structure su travail à Damas en 1927, Type d'enquête sociographique," *Opera Minora* (1963). See also Abdul-Karim Rafeq, "Craft Organization, Work Ethics and the Strains of Change in Ottoman Syria," *Journal of American Oriental Society* 111 (1991): 495–511.

12   For the changing role of this Mediterranean city see Thomas Philipp, *Acre: the Rise and Fall of a Palestinian City, 1730–1831* (New York: Columbia University Press, 2001).

13   Charles Issawi, *The Fertile Crescent, 1800–1914: A Documentary Economic History* (Oxford, UK: Oxford University Press, 1988). Leila Fawaz, *Merchants and Migrants in Nineteenth Century Beirut* (Cambridge, Mass.: Harvard University Press, 1983). Roger Owen, *The Middle East in the World Economy,* 2nd ed. (London: I.B. Tauris, 1993). Zouhair Ghazzal, *L'economie politique de Damas durant de XIXème Siècle: structures traditionelles et capitalisme* (Damascus: Institut français de Damas, 1993).

14   Michael Bonine, "The Introduction of Railroads in the Eastern Mediterranean: Their Economic and Social Impact in Syria," in *The Syrian Land: Processes of Integration and Fragmentation,* ed. Thomas Philipp and Birgit Schaebler (Stuttgart: F. Steiner, 1998).

15   Linda Schilcher, "The Impact of the Railways on the Grain Trade of Southern Syria, 1890–1925," in *The Syrian Land: Processes of Integration and Fragmentation.*

16   I have given short shrift to the details of the peasant hardships and uprisings so well documented by Linda Schilcher in a series of articles. See her "The Grain Economy of Late Ottoman Syria and the Issue of Large-Scale Commercialization" in *Landholding and Commercial Agriculture in the Ottoman Empire,* ed. Faruk Tabak and Caglar Keydar (Albany: SUNY Press, 1991), 173–95; "The Hauran Conflicts of the 1860s: A Chapter in the Rural History of Modern Syria," *International Journal of Middle East Studies* 13 (1981): 159–79; "The Impact of the Great Depression on Late Ottoman Syria," *New Perspectives on Turkey* 5–6 (1991): 167–89; and "Violence in Rural Syria in the 1880s and 1890s: State Centralization, Rural Integration and the World Market," in *Peasants and Politics in the Modern Middle East,* ed. Farhad Kazemi and John Waterbury (Miami: Florida International, 1991), 50–84. See also Abdallah Hanna, *Harakat al-'Amma al-Dimashqiyya fi al Qarnayn al- Thamin 'Ashar wa al-Tasi' 'Ashar* (Beirut: Ibn Khaldun, 1985).

17   The probate inventory document provides a glimpse of the juridical kin relations and the objects of consumption and tools of production of everyday life. A presentation of the deceased's name, place of residence, and his or her heirs introduces the document. There follows a list of the items that comprise the estate, starting with clothing and household effects. The items of the inventory are listed in a matrix-like array across and down the page. The name of the item is inscribed with its worth in piasters or *qurush* centered directly beneath it in a small, downward-pointing triangle. Arithmetic calculations are pushed to the side of the page. If the deceased's estate consists in considerable part of tools, farm animals, books, or jewels, these might well be listed and summed in a separate section. If the deceased owned a store, workshop, or warehouse, there follows a detailed inventory of its contents. Finally, if the deceased was drawing a salary, or held significant amounts of cash, these are listed and enumerated.

18   The late war years were, of course, characterized by rampant inflation and famine due to the imposition by the state of unbacked

paper money in Damascus, but the inflation discussed here is not that eighteenfold rise in the cost of living between 1914 and 1918 documented by the Ottoman Public Debt Administration. See S. B. Himadeh, *The Monetary and Banking System of Syria* (Beirut: American Press, 1935). Pamuk, *A Monetary History of the Ottoman Empire,* 224. The inflation documented in the estates of people who died in the 1910s is of an earlier era and due to different causes. See Haim Gerber and Nachum Gross, "Inflation or Deflation in Nineteenth Century Syria and Palestine," *Journal of Economic History* 40, no. 2 (1980). And Dominique Chevallier, "Western Development and Eastern Crisis in the Mid-Nineteenth Century: Syria Confronted with the European Economy," in William Roe Polk and Richard L. Chambers, eds., *Beginnings of Modernization in the Middle East: The Nineteenth Century* (Chicago: University of Chicago Press, 1968), 427.

19   See the classic formulation in Philip Khoury, *Urban Notables and Arab Nationalism* (Cambridge, UK: Cambridge University Press, 1983), 26–28. For more information on land tenure see James Reilly, "Properties around Damascus," *Arabica* 37 (1990): 90–114; "Shari'a Court Registers and Land Tenure around Nineteenth Century Damascus," *Middle East Studies Association Bulletin* 21 (1987): 155–69; "Property, Status and Class in Ottoman Damascus: Case Studies from the Nineteenth Century," *Journal of the American Oriental Society* 112 (1992): 9–21; "Status Groups and Property Holding in the Damascus Hinterland 1828–1880," *International Journal of Middle East Studies* 21 (1989): 517–39.

20   Commercial inventories are listed separately from commercial real estate, which rarely appears in the record since most retail and wholesale commercial premises were leased from *waqf* endowments. When private commercial property is listed, it is almost never appraised. Women were highly unlikely to have commercial inventories as assets. In the 1880s sample, only three did, and in the 1910s sample only one woman did.

21   Although I am convinced that social class is a key category, I shall avoid that term with its connotations of identity and inflexibility of membership and refer for the time being instead to the analytically generated wealth strata revealed by dividing the samples into submedian, intermediate (between the median and the average), and super-average groups based on their gross probated assets.

22 The distribution of this cash among women of the different strata shows a different pattern from that of men between the two time periods. In the earlier period, superaverage women held the vast majority (87 percent) of the 5 percent of cash in women's estates, middle women held a modest 13 percent, and submedian women held none. By the 1910s, the holdings of the mere 2 percent of liquidity held by women were somewhat differently distributed. Superaverage women held only 71 percent, the poorest women held 3 percent, and more than a quarter (26 percent) was held by women in the middle of the sample— twice the percentage they had held previously. Unlike the middle stratum of men, whose per capita holdings and total share of the cash declined, middle-stratum women held more cash in the new decade.

23 Gerber and Gross, "Inflation or Deflation."

24 Even if interest-bearing transactions were commonplace, when debt and credit appear in the Islamic court records it was with the understanding that the return on a loan of money is a dividend share of profits or the privilege of incurring obligation from the debtor.

25 Since debting decreases the most among the submedian strata, the group most likely to need debt for survival, this can be attributed to a reluctance among potential lenders to invest in loans that might be repaid in inflated, devalued currency. As liquidity increases, debt bonds become an unattractive proposition, and non-kin publicly recorded social obligations decrease.

26 James Reilly, "From Workshops to Sweatshops: Damascus Textiles and the World Economy in the Last Ottoman Century," *Review Fernand Braudel Center,* 16, no. 2 (1993): 199–213, also "Damascus Merchants and Trade in the Transition to Capitalism," *Canadian Journal of History* 27, no. 1 (1992): 1–27. For the structure and ritual of guilds, see Elias Qudsi, *Notices sur les Corporations de Damas* (Leiden: Carlo Landberg, 1885).

27 Annelies Moors, *Women, Property and Islam: Palestinian Experiences 1920–1990* (Cambridge, UK: Cambridge University Press, 1995).

28 Peter Sluglett and Marion Farouk Sluglett, "The Application of the 1858 Land Code in Greater Syria: Some Preliminary Observations," in *Land Tenure and Social Transformation in the Middle East,* ed. Tarif Khalidi (Beirut: American University of Beirut Press, 1984).

29 For changes in succession and land tenure (and alternate datings) around this period see Robert Eisenman, "The Young Turk Legisla-

tion, 1913–1917, and Its Application in Palestine/Israel," in David Kushner, *Palestine in the Late Ottoman Period* (Jerusalem: Brill, 1986), 59–73.

30   United States National Archives (USNA) Consular Records, Damascus, July 14, 1903.

Chapter Five

1   Beshara Doumani, ed., "Introduction," in *Family History in the Middle East: Household, Property and Gender* (Albany: State University of New York Press, 2003), 1.

2   The traditional *fada'il* literature that praises a particular city includes not just chapters on who entered or conquered the city, but chapters on who is buried in the city. The *yawmiyat* journals often run on for pages about which travelers or dignitaries arrived and left on a particular day, and in particular, include many entries on who died. The biographical dictionaries, a classical Islamic genre, preserve history in the form of entries for the city's notables. See Muhammad Jamil al-Shatti, *Rawd al-Bashar fi A'yan Dimashq fi al-Qarn al-Thalith 'Ashar* (Damascus: Dar al-Basha'ir, 1994).

3   For views of Damascene family life, see *The Memoirs of Muhammad Kurd 'Ali: A Selection,* Khalil Totah (trans.) (Washington: American Council of Learned Societies, 1954), 1–11. Ahmad Ibish, *Dafatir Shamiyya 'Atiqa* (Damascus: Kotaiba, 2002) contains fragments of oral history on marriage, daily life, and inheritance from Fatima Badiwi, who lived during the period in question; also see Ahmad Hilmi 'Allaf, *Dimashq fi Matl'a al-Qarn al-'Ishrin* (Damascus: Wizarat al-Thaqafa, 1976). An excellent secondary introduction to premodern customs can be found in Yusuf Jamil Na'isa, *Mujtama' Madinat Dimashq 1772–1840,* 2 vols. (Damascus: Tlas, 1982).

4   Erika Friedl, "Tribal Enterprises and Marriage Issues in Twentieth Century Iran," in Doumani (ed.), *Family History,* 152.

5   Jack Goody, *Bridewealth and Dowry* (Cambridge, UK: Cambridge University Press, 1973), 37.

6   The most important cultural construction of the family came through the *shari'a* courts—especially the probate *qassam* court. Doumani and Agmon have each described the mutual construction of family and court through litigation cases; the *mukhallafat* documents present family more as a structure. See Beshara Doumani, "Endowing Family *Waqf:* Property, Devolution and Gender in Greater Syria,

1800–1860," *Comparative Studies in Society and History* 40, no. 1 (1998): 3–41; and Iris Agmon, *Family and Court: Legal Culture and Modernity in Late Ottoman Palestine* (Syracuse, N.Y.: Syracuse University Press, 2005).

7   Fargues presents a useful hypothesis to keep in mind based on his study of a nineteenth-century Egyptian census: The more variable families are in practice, the more weight is loaded on culturally constructed discourses of the family that present them as stable and durable. Fargues observes, "A paradox: the family is as stable as an institution as it is ephemeral as a grouping." Philip Fargues, "Family and Household in Nineteenth Century Cairo," in Doumani (ed.) *Family History*, 45.

8   Noel Coulson, *Succession in the Muslim Family* (Cambridge, UK: Cambridge University Press, 1971).

9   Annelies Moors, *Women, Property and Islam: Palestinian Experiences 1920–1990* (Cambridge, UK: Cambridge University Press, 1995).

10   See Randi Deguilhem, ed., *Le Waqf dans l'espace islamique; outil de pouvoir socio-politique* (Damascus: IFEAD, 1995), and Doumani, "Endowing Family *Waqf,*" 3–41.

11   Khaled Chatila, *Le Mariage chez les Musulmanes en Syrie: étude de sociologie* (Paris: Paul Geuthner, 1934).

12   Based on a survey of marriage contracts registered with the Damascus courts between 1902 and 1920 in which 84 percent of marriages were contracted with *mu'akhars* that were exactly half of their corresponding *muqadam* or up-front bridal gift, I will proceed on the assumption that the ratio of the two parts of the marriage gift is fairly stable, and thus that the *mu'akhar* may stand in for the whole marriage payment. See also Kazim Daghestani, *Etude sociologique sur la famille musulmane contemporaine en Syrie* (Paris: 1932).

13   Goody, *Bridewealth and Dowry;* and G. P. Murdock, "Ethnographic Atlas," *World Cultures* 2, no. 4 (1986).

14   Evolutionary biologists predict globally rare dowry or "female competition" for wealthy mates to occur in stratified societies of limited polygyny, a situation that applies to the late Ottoman Islamic world as well as to some bird species but cannot be elaborated here. Steven Gaulin and James Boster, "Dowry as Female Competition," *American Anthropologist* 92, no. 4 (1990).

15   For an interesting but unsuccessful attempt to economize *mahr,* see Ivy Papps, "The Role and Determinants of Bride-Price: The Case of a

Palestinian Village," *Current Anthropology* 24, no. 2 (1983). For a more sophisticated exchange see also Alice Schlegel and Rohn Eloul, "Marriage Transactions: Labor, Property, Status," *American Anthropologist* 90, no. 2 (1988); Mildred Dickemann, "Women, Class and Dowry," *American Anthropologist* 93, no. 4 (1991); Mildred Dickemann, "Dowry Disputes: A Reply to Schlegel," *American Anthropologist* 95, no. 1 (1993); and Alice Schlegel, "Dowry: Who Competes for What?" *American Anthropologist* 95, no. 1 (1993).

16   Judith Tucker, "Marriage and Family in Nablus, 1720–1856: Towards a History of Arab Muslim Marriage," *Journal of Family History* 13, no. 1 (1988), pp. 165–79.

17   Benedict Anderson, *Imagined Communities: Reflections on the Origin and Spread of Nationalism* (London: Verso, 1983).

18   Chatila, *Le Mariage*, 188ff.

19   For example, see Elizabeth Frierson, "Mirrors Out, Mirrors In: Domestication and the Rejection of the Foreign in Late Ottoman Women's Magazines (1875–1908)," in *Women, Patronage and Self-Representation in Islamic Societies*, ed. D. Fairchild Ruggles (Albany: SUNY Press, 2000).

20   It would be easy to assume that these poor, familyless women of the war years were a new class of dead produced by World War I, and some of them certainly were, but most who died prior to 1917 and some who died subsequently had already failed to marry and have children prior to the famine. Their modest estates were brought to probate courtesy of their primary heir, the state.

21   Men take women from the level above them, so liquidity circulates from the bottom to the top and women circulate from the top to the bottom, as in Claude Levi-Strauss, *Anthropologie structurale* (Chicago: University of Chicago Press, 1983). E. R. Leach, *Rethinking Anthropology* (London: Athlone Press, 1971).

22   The idea of heritage and prestige as "dowry" goes along with the twentieth-century trope that "women are the custodians of tradition." See, for example, Esther Meir-Glitzenstein, "Our Dowry: Identity and Memory among Iraqi Immigrants in Israel," *Middle Eastern Studies* 38, 2 (2002), which has nothing to do with marriage payments, everything to do with heritage. This idea should illuminate the field of the "commodification of heritage" which remains suggestively descriptive by focusing only on consumption habits as indicators of static class identity and not on the strategic recombination and mar-

ket movement in marriage. Christa Salamandra, *A New Old Damascus: Authenticity and Distinction in Urban Syria* (Bloomington: University of Indiana Press, 2004), addresses the issue of women's bodies and public and private space.

23 For a contemporary study of the fluctuation in popularity of "token" *mahr* see Herman Turk and Qablan Majali, "Culture and Markets in Jordanian Bride Prices: On the Diffusion of Tradition," *Sociological Abstracts* (1989).

Chapter Six

1   *Markaz lil Watha'iq al-Tarikhiyya (MWT)*, Damascus Series Sijills 1226/101; 1226/125; 1456/35; 1468/46; 1468/141; 1093/3; 1093/25; 1093/66; 1093/96; 1093/114; 1093/152B; 1119/24; 1119/26; 1119/37; 1119/39; 1119/43; 757/8; 808/87; 795/81; 795/90; 872/28; 878/111; 926/15; 926/96; 953/113; 953/146; 953/151; 1000/57; 1001/29; 1001/124; 1001/128; 1040B/39; 1053/62; 1055/61; 1055/65. This includes more *sijills* than were used in previous sampling.

2   See chapter 4 of this volume.

3   On Damascus publishing, see Iskandar Luqa, *Al-Harakah al-Adabiyya fi Dimashq 1800–1918* (Damascus: Matabi' Alif Ba al-Adib, 1976).

4   On other issues relating to the *'ulama* of Damascus, see John Voll, "The Non-Wahhabi Hanbalis of Eighteenth Century Syria," *American Journal of Arabic Studies* 3 (1975): 48–59, and H. Fleischer, "Miha'il Mesaka's Cultur-Statistik von Damaskus," *Kleinere Schriften* 3 (Leipzig, 1885): 306–40, and his "Briefwechsel zwischen den Anführern der Wahhabiten und dem Pasa von Damascus," *Zeitschrift der Deutschen Morganländischen Gesellschaft* 11 (1857).

5   See Dale Eickelman, "The Art of Memory: Islamic Education and Its Social Reproduction," *Comparative Studies in Society and History* 20 (1978): 485–516, and Brinkley Messick, *The Calligraphic State: Textual Domination and History in a Muslim Society* (Berkeley: University of California Press, 1993).

6   Sheikh Khalid Naqshbandi wrote a commentary on this work.

7   See R. A. Nicholson, *A Literary History of the Arabs* (Cambridge, UK: Cambridge University Press, 1966), and A. J. Arberry, *Le Soufisme: introduction à la mystique de l'Islam,* trans. Jean Gouillard (Paris: Éditions des Cahiers du sud, 1952), and J. Spencer Trimingham, *The Sufi Orders in Islam* (Oxford, UK: Clarendon Press, 1971).

8   Trimingham, *Sufi Orders,* 223.

9   For background on early Ottoman Egypt see P. M. Holt, *Egypt and the Fertile Crescent 1516–1922* (Ithaca, N.Y.: Cornell University Press, 1966), and Michael Winter, *Egyptian Society under Ottoman Rule 1517-1798* (London: Routledge, 1992). See Michael Winter, *Society and Religion in Early Ottoman Egypt: Studies in the Writings of Abd al-Wahhab al-Sharani* (New Brunswick, N.J.: Transaction Books, 1982), 47–50, and 'Abd al-Wahab al-Sha'rani, *Lata'if al-Minan wal Akhlaqfi Wujub al-Tahaduth bi Na'mat Allah 'ala al-Itlaq* (Cairo: 'Alam al-Fikr, 1976), vol. 2, 158–60, for descriptions.

10 Many of Sharani's works seem to have been published in 1277 AH and 1278 AH, with another set of editions dating from about 1300 AH.

11 *MWT*, Damascus Series, Sijill 1119.

12 He might have studied with Kuzbari and Tantawi, as so many Shafi'is of Damascus did.

13 See David Commins, *Islamic Reform: Politics and Social Change in Late Ottoman Syria* (New York: Oxford University Press), 30–40, on Khani's friendship with Qasimi.

14 See Commins, *Islamic Reform*, 34–38, and 'Ala al-Din al-Khani, *Al-Usra al Khaniyya al-Dimashqiyya* (Damascus, n.d.).

15 *MWT*, Damascus Series, Sijill 1119.

16 Muhammad Jamil al-Shatti, *Rawd al-Bashar fi A'yan Dimashq fi al-Qarn al-Thalith 'Ashar* (Damascus: Dar al-Basha'ir, 1994), 376–77.

17 On 'Abd al-Qader al-Jaza'iri, see, for example, Michel Chodkiewicz, James Chrestensen, et al., *The Spiritual Writings of Abd al- Qader al-Jazairi* (Albany: State University of New York Press, 1995).

18 Itzchak Weismann, *Taste of Modernity: Sufism, Salafiyya, and Arabism in Late Ottoman Damascus* (Leiden: Brill, 2001), 193–260.

19 Rainer Hermann, *Kulturkrise und konservative Erneuerung: Muhammad Kurd Ali (1876–1953) und das geistige Leben in Damascus zu Beginn des 20. Jahrhunderts* (Frankfurt: Lang, 1989), 26–39, and Joseph Escovitz, "He Was the Muhammad Abduh of Syria: A Study of Tahir al-Jaza'iri and His Influence," *International Journal of Middle East Studies* 18 (1986), 293–310.

20 See Commins, *Islamic Reform*, 37, and al-Shatti, *Rawd al-Bashar,* 386. Ahmad Khani who fought for and won leadership of the branch with As'ad al-Sahib's help was financially dissolute and engaged in strategic

madhhab switching, finding it politic in the 1870s to forsake Shafi'ism and become a Hanafi in order to more easily acquire judicial posts.

21 Commins, *Islamic Reform,* 45.

22 See 'Abd al-Hamid al-Zahrawi, *Al-Fiqh wal-Tasawwuf* (Cairo: al-Maktab al-Fanni lil-Nashr, 1901).

23 This account of the *"mujtahids* incident" is taken from Commins, *Islamic Reform,* 35–47. For more on this and other aspects of Jamal al-Din al-Qasimi, see Weismann, *Taste of Modernity,* 276–82, and Zafir al-Qasimi, *Jamal al-Din al-Qasimi wa 'Asruh* (Damascus: Maktab Atlas, 1965), 43–69.

24 See Leila Hudson, "Reading al-Sha'rani: The Sufi Genealogy of Islamic Modernism in Late Ottoman Damascus," *Journal of Islamic Studies* 15, no. 1 (2004): 39–68.

25 For much more on the practices and history of the Khalidiyya in Damascus, see Weismann, *Taste of Modernity,* 31–80.

26 Darwish was one of the names that had dropped out of the second sample of probate inventories. See chapter 3.

27 Weismann, *Taste of Modernity,* 123–40.

28 His manuscript has been published by Jacob Landau, *The Hejaz Railway and the Muslim Pilgrimage* (Detroit, Mich.: Wayne State University Press, 1971).

Chapter Seven

1   Donald Blaisdell, *European Financial Control in the Ottoman Empire* (New York: Columbia University Press, 1929), 74–107.

2   Engin Akarli, "Abdulhamid II's Attempt to Integrate Arabs into the Ottoman Sytem," in David Kushner, *Palestine in the Late Ottoman Period* (Jerusalem: Brill, 1986), 74–92; and Selim Deringil, *The Well Protected Domains: Ideology and Legitimation of Power in the Ottoman Empire 1876–1909* (London: I.B. Tauris, 1998), 16–41.

3   See Comte Cressaty, *La Syrie française,* 23 (Paris, 1915) and for other examples E. G. Rey, *Essai sur la domination française en Syrie durant le Moyen-Age* (Paris: Imprimerie Thunot & Cie, 1866) and Henry Richard, *La Syrie et la guerre* (Paris: Chapelot, 1916).

4   On French educational policy in Syria, see J. P. Spagnolo, "French Influence in Syria Prior to World War I: The Functional Weakness of Imperialism," *Middle East Journal* 23, no. 1 (1969): 45–42; Randi Deguilhem, "Idées française et enseignement ottoman: l'école secondaire Maktab Anbar à Damas," *Revue du monde musulman et de la Méditerranée* 52, no. 3 (1989): 198–206. Also Jacques Thobie, *Intérèts et imperialisme français dans l'Empire Ottoman 1895–1914* (Paris: Imprimerie Nationale, 1977).

5   William Shorrock, "The Origin of the French Mandate in Syria and Lebanon: The Railroad Question, 1901–1914," *International Journal of Middle East Studies* 1, no. 2 (1970): 133–53.

6   The definitive source on the French railroads in Syria and Lebanon is Eleuthere Elefteriades, *Les Chemins de fer en Syrie et au Liban* (Beirut: Imprimerie Catholique, 1944).

7   On 'Izzat see Caesar Farah, "Arab Supporters of 'Abdulhamid II: 'Izzet al-'Abid," in *Archivum Ottomanicum* (Wiesbaden: Otto Harrasowitz, 1997), 189–220, and Ruth Roded, "Social Patterns among the Urban Elite of Syria during the Late Ottoman Period 1876–1918," in Kushner, *Palestine in the Late Ottoman Period,* 155–57.

8   Although he was instrumental to the Sultan 'Abdulhamid in an early campaign against the Committee of Union and Progress movement, he was not present at the time of the revolution in July 1908, having

been replaced in March 1906. He was reappointed in December 1908 after the revolution.

9   See Stefan Weber, "Der Marja-Platz in Damaskus: Entstehung Eines Modernen Stadtzentrums Unter den Osmanen als Ausdruck Einen Strukturellen Wandels," *Damaszener Mitteilungen* 10 (1998): 291–344.

10 Abdul-Karim Rafeq, *Tarikh al-Jamiʿa al-Suriyya al-Bidaya wal-Namu 1901–1946* (Damascus: Maktaba Nobel, 2004), 9–30.

11 For a comprehensive overview of the educational landscape in late Ottoman Damascus, see Randi Deguilhem, "State Civil Education in Late Ottoman Damascus: A Unifiying or a Separating Force," in Thomas Philipp and Birgit Schaebler (eds.), *The Syrian Land: Processes of Integration and Fragmentation in Bilad al-Sham from the 18th to the 20th Century* (Stuttgart: Franz Steiner, 1998), 221–50. For an especially clear portrait of the Christian schools in the 1870s, see Nuʿman Qasatli, *Al-Rawdat al-Ghina fi Dimashq al-Fayha* (Beirut: Dar al-Raid al-ʿArabi, 1982), 117–20.

12 Randi Deguilhem-Schoem, "Idées françaises et enseignement ottoman: l'école secondaire Maktab ʿAnbar à Damas," *Revue du monde musulman et de la Méditerranee* 52/53 (1989): 199–206. For a firsthand account of the school credited with educating the first generation of Arab nationalists, see Zafir al-Qasimi, *Maktab ʿAnbar: Suwar wa Dhikrayyat min Hayatina al-Thaqafiyya wal-Siyasiyya wal-Ijtimaʿiyya* (Beirut: al-Matbaʿa al-Kathulukiyya, 1964).

13 Randi Deguilhem, "A Revolution in Learning? The Islamic Contribution to the Ottoman State Schools: Examples from the Syrian Provinces," in Ali Çaksu (ed.), *Proc. International Congress on Learning and Education in the Ottoman World* (Istanbul: Research Centre for Islamic History, Art and Culture, 2001), 285–96.

14 For an overview of the centrality of the Hamidian education program see Benjamin Fortna, *Islam, the State and Education in the Late Ottoman Empire* (Oxford, UK: Oxford University Press, 2002), 113–29 and particularly 130–64 on "Buildings and Discipline." And for its sociology within Damascus see Roded, "Social Patterns," 146ff.

15 Dar Hayal, *Forty Four Months in Constantinople* (London, 1918).

16 British Foreign Office 195/2024 (FO 195/2024) Damascus, no. 55, November 10, 1898.

17 Ibid.

18 Ibid.

19 Ibid.

20   Ibid.

21   The British Consul Richards made special note of the cordiality of relations between the emperor and the Damascus governor, as ever with a precise eye for the rival power's developing relations with this important Ottoman province.

22   FO 195/2024.

23   See William Ochsenwald, *The Hijaz Railway* (Charlotte: University of Virginia, 1980). For a contemporary view see Muhammad Kurd 'Ali, "Sikkat al-Hijaz," *al-Muqtataf* 29 (1904): 970–80.

24   Jacob Landau, *The Hejaz Railway and the Muslim Pilgrimage* (Detroit, Mich.: Wayne State University Press, 1971).

25   Farah, "Arab Supporters."

26   On 'Izzat's local projects and their perception see Martin Hartmann, *Reisebriefe Aus Syrien* (Berlin: Dietrich Reimer, 1913), 18–19. The 'Ayn Fijeh project was initially assigned to Hijaz Railway engineers as an aspect of their project and financed with a tax on imported kerosene. But the railway was unable to undertake the project, and in October 1906 it was contracted to the local firm of a Damascene Christian living in Alexandria. The waters of the 'Ayn Fijeh spring outside Damascus were connected by pipeline to a newly constructed underground reservoir at al-Salihiyya, which was to become the main water source for the city. The reservoir at al-Salihiyya was inaugurated in July 1907, although it was not completed until spring 1908. This water was pumped to about two hundred public fountains around the city and was to become the main water source for the city. The fountain in front of the new Serail was designed as a symbol of Abdulhamid's thirty-third anniversary in September of 1908, but it came to be associated, like the Hijaz Railway, with the Young Turk era. Eventually the 'Ayn Fijeh project would become a publicly held local company.

27   Muhammad Husni, *Kitab Muntakhabat al-Tawarikh li Dimashq*, Kamal Salibi (ed.), 3 vols. (Beirut: al-Matba' al-Hadithah, 1979), 276.

28   Gertrude Bell, *The Desert and Sown* (London: Heinemann, 1907), 141–42.

29   Roded, "Social Patterns," 161.

30   FO 6118/3 Quarterly Report from Damascus (draft), October-December 1912.

31   FO 6118/3 Quarterly Report from Damascus (draft), January-March 1913.

32   FO 6118/3 Quarterly Report from Damascus (draft), April-June 1904.

33   FO 6118/3 Quarterly Report from Damascus, July-September 1908, enclosure "Public Feeling in Damascus as Regards the Constitution."

34   FO 6118/3, Damascus, August 12, 1908, Quarterly Report from Damascus, "State of Affairs in Damascus Relating to the New Regime," Damascus, August 12 ,1908.

35   FO 6118/3, August 22, 1908, Quarterly Report from Damascus, "Continued Rejoicings at the Restitution of the Constitution and State of Local Affairs," August 22, 1908.

36   FO 6118/3, September 4, 1908, Quarterly Report from Damascus, "State of Affairs in Damascus as to the New Regime," September 4, 1908.

37   FO 6118/3, Quarterly Report from Damascus, July-September 1908.

38   FO 6118/3 Quarterly Report from Damascus, October 10, 1908, "Protest to Foreign Ministers against Bulgaria and Austria for Violation of Berlin Treaty," October 10, 1908.

39   *Al-Muqtabas: Jaridah Yawmiyyah Siyasiyyah, Iqtisadiyya, Ijtima iyya* (Damascus: al-Muqtabas, 1908/1909).

Chapter Eight

1   Martin Hartmann, *Reisebriefe Aus Syrien* (Berlin: Dietrich Reimer, 1913), 18–19.

2   Ruth Roded, "Social Patterns among the Urban Elite of Syria during the Late Ottoman Period 1876–1918," in David Kushner, *Palestine in the Late Ottoman Period* (Jerusalem: Brill, 1986), 155–57.

3   William Ochsenwald, *The Hijaz Railway* (Charlotte: University of Virginia, 1980), 130.

4   Hasan Kayali, *Arabs and Young Turks: Ottomanism, Arabism and Islamism in the Ottoman Empire 1908–1918* (Berkeley: University of California Press, 1997), 151.

5   Donald Cioeta, "Ottoman Censorship in Lebanon and Syria, 1876–1908," *International Journal of Middle East Studies* 10 (1979): 387–407.

6   Much of Rashid Khalidi's early work illustrates this emergence of a discursive Arab identity in the debates about turkification. See, for example, his "The 1912 Election Campaign in the Cities of Bilad al-Sham," *International Journal of Middle East Studies* 16 (November 1984): 461–474; and "The Press as a Source for Modern Arab Political History," *Arab Studies Quarterly* 3 (Winter 1981): 22–42. See also, Hasan Kayali, "Elections and the Electoral Process in the Ottoman Empire, 1876–1919," *International Journal of Middle East Studies* 27 (August 1995): 256–286; and Erol Ulker, "Contextualizing 'Turkification': Nation-Building in the Late Ottoman Empire, 1908–1918," *Nations and Nationalism* 11, no. 4 (2005): 613–36.

7   These participants in the Paris-based journal *Correspondence d'Orient* and the Paris Congress of 1913 were prolific writers in French. Negib Azoury on the left wrote *Le réveil de la nation arabe dans l'Asie turque* (Paris: Plon-Nourrit, 1905), which may have been the first use of the "Arab Awakening" theme later made famous by George Antonius. The rightist Nadra Moutron made the case for a French Lebanon and Syria in *La Syrie de demain* (Paris: Plon-Nourrit, 1916), while George Samne analyzed the particular aspects of the situation in a series of

pamphlets and articles published in Paris in 1919 and 1920 with the titles "Le Cherifat de la Mecque et l'unité syrienne," "L'éffort Syrien pendant la guerre," "Les oeuvres français en Syrie," "Le Liban autonome," and "La Question sioniste."

8 Itzchak Weismann, *Taste of Modernity: Sufism, Salafiyya, and Arabism in Late Ottoman Damascus* (Leiden: Brill, 2001), 132–40.

9 Muhammad Kurd 'Ali, *Khitat al-Sham*, vol. 6, 142 (Damascus: Matba'at al Taraqqi, 1950).

10 The joint Ottoman-German military mission was doomed from the start and required a new "desert ration'" consisting of 1 kilogram of biscuits, dates, olives, and a gourdful of water. The plan required 11,000 transport camels and 25,000 men to cross the desert in summer. It ended in disaster. Further defeats at Gaza and the deterioration of the Mesopotamian arena resulted in constantly stretched military resources. The Ylderim lightning brigade under German General von Falkynheim further undermined the Syrian Fourth Army situation. See Djemal Pasha, *Memories of a Turkish Statesman 1913–1919* (New York: Arno, 1973).

11 For the negotiations between the rival DHP and Hijaz railways see Ochsenwald, *Hijaz Railway*, and Max L. Gross, "Ottoman Rule in the Province of Damascus 1860–1909" (PhD diss., Georgetown University, 1979).

12 His secretary remembers that death threats were common currency in Jamal's administration. Geoffrey Lewis, "An Ottoman Officer in Palestine 1914–1918," in Kushner, *Palestine in the Late Ottoman Period*, 404–5.

13 The architect was Max Zürcher, whose sister Josephine left memoirs of the period. See Uarda Frutiger, *Ärtzin im Orient Auch Wenn's dem Sultan Nicht Gefällt: Josephina Th. Zürcher 1866–1932* (Basel: Schwabe, 1987), 135–36.

14 Carl Watzinger, *Theodor Wiegand: Ein Deutscher Archaeologe 1864–1936* (Munich: C. H. Beck, 1944), 273.

15 See P. Clemen, *Kunstschutz im Kriege, Berichte über dem Zustand der Kunstdenkmäler auf den verschiedenen Kriegsschauplätzen* (Leipzig: EA Seeman, 1919), for similar efforts to salvage artistic capital on the Western front.

16 Theodor Wiegand, *Halbmond im Letzten Viertel, Briefe und Reiseberichte aus der alten Türkei von Theodor und Marie Wiegand 1895 bis 1918* (Munich: Bruckmann, 1970), 198–200.

17 Wiegand, *Halbmond,* 216.

18 Ibid., 299. This classic work is C. Watzinger and K. Wulzinger, *Damaskus: Die Antike Stadt* (Berlin: Vereinigung Wissenschaftlicher Verbeger, 1921).

19 Wiegand, *Halbmond,* 302.

20 Djemal Pasha, *Memories of a Turkish Statesman, 1913–1919* (New York: Arno, 1973); *La vérité sur la question syrienne* (Istanbul: Tanine, 1916); Muhammad Kurd 'Ali, *al-Mudhakkirat,* vol. 1 (Damascus: Matba'at al-Turki, 1948), 107–10; and George Antonius, *The Arab Awakening: The Story of the Arab National Movement* (New York: G. P. Putnam's Sons, 1946), 175–89.

21 Maxime Nicholas, "Questions monétaires en Syrie," PhD Thesis, University of Lyon (Lyon, France, 1921), pp. 13 and 24. See also, Christopher Clay, "Origins of Modern Banking in the Levant: The Branch Network of the Imperial Ottoman Bank 1890-1914," *International Journal of Middle East Studies* 26(1994): 589–614; and Charles Issawi, *An Economic History of the Middle East and North Africa* (New York: Columbia University Press, 1982).

22 Ulrich Trumpener, *Germany and the Ottoman Empire, 1914–1918* (Princeton, N.J.: Princeton University Press, 1968), 21 ff.

23 Wiegand, *Halbmond,* 248.

24 Ibid., 229.

25 Maxime Nicolas, "Questions monétaires en Syrie," 45.

26 Antonius, *The Arab Awakening,* 241; Halide Edib, *Memoirs of Halide Edib* (New York: Century, n.d.), 450–51; and Linda Schilcher, "The Famine of 1915–1918 in Greater Syria," in *Problems of the Modern Middle East in Historical Perspective: Essays in Honour of Albert Hourani,* ed. John Spagnolo (Reading, UK: Ithaca Press for Middle East Center, St. Anthony's College, Oxford, 1992).

27 For details of the exchanges-in-kind of grain that benefited Jamal and his partners, see Fritz Grobba, *Bericht Über die Wirtschaftliche Lage in Damaskus im März und April 1918 und über Grosszugige Getreide-Verträge turk. Beamten und Offiziere* (unpublished, Damascus, 1918).

28 Ibid.

29 Joseph Massad, *Colonial Effects: The Making of National Identity in Jordan* (New York: Columbia, 2001); and Mary Wilson, *King Abdullah, Britain and the Making of Jordan* (Cambridge, UK: Cambridge University Press, 1987); and C. Ernest Dawn, *From Ottomanism to Arabism: Essays on the Origin of Arab Nationalism* (Urbana: University of Illinois Press, 1973).

30 S. C. Rolls, *Steel Chariots in the Desert: The Story of an Armoured-Car Driver with the Duke of Westminster in Libya and in Arabia with T. E. Lawrence* (London: J. Cape, 1937), 165–66.

31 Ibid., 275.

32 Ibid., 256.

33 Ibid., 261.

34 Ibid., 179.

35 Ibid., 148.

36 Ibid., 151.

37 Ibid., 165.

38 Ibid., 167.

39 Ibid., 275.

40 Ibid., 234.

Chapter Nine

1   Bourdieu's habitus is famously if opaquely defined as "systems of durable, transposable dispositions, structured structures predisposed to function as structuring structures, that is, as principles of the generation and structuring of practice which can be objectively 'regulated' and 'regular' without in any way being the product of obedience to rules, objectively adapted to their goals without presupposing a conscious aiming at ends or an express mastery of the operations necessary to attain them and, being all this, collectively orchestrated without being the product of the orchestrating action of a conductor."

2   Benjamin Lee and Edward LiPuma, "Cultures of Circulation: The Imaginations of Modernity," *Public Culture* 14, no. 1 (2002): 191–213.

3   Albert Hourani, "Ottoman Reform and the Politics of Notables," in William Roe Polk and Richard L. Chambers, eds., *Beginnings of Modernization in the Middle East: The Nineteenth Century* (Chicago: University of Chicago Press, 1968), 49.

4   Linda Schatkowski Schilcher, *Families in Politics: Damascene Factions and Estates of the 18th and 19th Centuries* (Stuttgart, Germany: Franz Steiner Verlag, 1985); Philip Khoury, *Urban Notables and Arab Nationalism* (Cambridge, UK: Cambridge University Press, 1983).

5   Hourani, "Ottoman Reform," 46.

INDEX